■ DRUGS
The Straight Facts

Birth Control Pills

DRUGS The Straight Facts

■ **DRUGS**
The Straight Facts

Birth
Control
Pills

Jon Zonderman and
Laurel Shader, M.D.

Consulting Editor
David J. Triggle
University Professor
School of Pharmacy and Pharmaceutical Sciences
State University of New York at Buffalo

CHELSEA HOUSE
P U B L I S H E R S
An imprint of Infobase Publishing

Birth Control Pills

Chelsea House
An imprint of Infobase Publishing
132 West 31st Street
New York NY 10001

Library of Congress Cataloging-in-Publication Data

Zonderman, Jon.
  Birth control pills / Jon Zonderman and Laurel Shader.
    p. cm. — (Drugs, the straight facts)
  Includes bibliographical references and index.
  ISBN 0-7910-8553-8 (hardcover)
  1. Oral contraceptives—Juvenile literature. I. Shader, Laurel. II. Title. III. Series.
  RG137.5.Z66 2006
  613.9'432—dc22   2006004994

Table of Contents

Drugs and Their Uses

For many thousands of years, humans have used a variety of agents to cure their ills, promote their well-being, relieve their misery, and control their fertility. Until the beginning of the twentieth century, these agents were all of natural origin, including many of plant origin as well as naturally occurring elements such as arsenic and antimony. The sixteenth century alchemist and physician known as Paracelsus used mercury and arsenic in his treatment of syphilis, worms, and other diseases that were extremely common at that time; his cure rates remain unknown. It is of interest, though, that arsenic trioxide is still used today, albeit in limited fashion, as an anticancer agent, and antimony derivatives are used in the treatment of the tropical disease leishmaniasis.

Our story of modern drug discovery begins with the German physician and scientist Paul Ehrlich. Born in 1854, Ehrlich became interested in the ways in which synthetic dyes, then becoming a major product of the German fine chemical industry, could selectively stain certain tissues and cellular components. He reasoned that such dyes might form the basis for drugs that would selectively interact with diseased cells and organisms. One of Ehrlich's early successes was the arsenical "606"—patented under the name Salvarsan—as a treatment for syphilis. Ehrlich's dream was to create the "magic bullet," a drug that would with absolute specificity target only the diseased cell or the disease-causing organism and not affect healthy tissues and cells. In this he was not successful, but his research did lay the groundwork for the subsequent great discoveries of the twentieth century, including the discovery of the sulfonamide drugs and the antibiotic penicillin. The latter agent saved countless lives during World War II.

From these original advances has come the vast array of drugs that are available to the modern physician. We are increasingly close to Ehrlich's aim of a magic bullet: Drugs can now target very specific molecular defects in a number of cancers, and doctors today have the ability to interrogate the human genome to more effectively match the drug with the patient. In the next one or two decades, it is almost certain that the cost of reading an individual genome will be sufficiently cheap that such "personalized" medicines will become the rule rather than the exception. These drugs do, however, carry very significant costs of both discovery and delivery, thus raising significant social issues of availability and equity of medical treatments.

Despite these current discoveries, it is interesting to note that a very significant fraction of the currently available drugs, notably antibiotics and anticancer agents, are either natural products or are derived from natural products. Such chemicals have been forged in the crucible of evolution and have presumably been derived by nature for very specific biological purposes.

The twenty-first century will continue to produce major advances in medicines and medicine delivery. Nature, however, is also a resilient foe. Diseases and organisms develop resistance to existing drugs so that new molecules must be constantly sought. This is particularly true for anti-infective and anticancer agents. Additionally, new and more lethal forms of existing diseases can rapidly develop and with the ease of travel can easily assume pandemic form. Hence the current concerns about avian flu. Also, diseases that have been previously dormant or geographically circumscribed may suddenly break out worldwide. In this way, for instance, an Ebola epidemic would produce many casualties. Finally, there are serious concerns for man-made epidemics through the deliberate spread of existing biological disease agents or through the introduction of a laboratory-manufactured or rejuvenated organism such as smallpox. It is therefore imperative that the search for new medicines continues.

All of us at some point in life will take a medicine, even if it is only aspirin for a headache. For some individuals, drug use will be constant throughout life, as in the current treatment of

AIDS, or will take place only during a certain stage, such as a woman taking hormonal contraceptives during her period of fertility. Quite generally, as we age we will likely be exposed to a variety of medications from childhood vaccines to pain-relieving drugs in a terminal disease. It is not easy to get accurate and understandable knowledge about the drugs that are used to treat diseases. There are, of course, highly specialized volumes and periodicals for the physician and scientist, but these demand a substantial knowledge basis and experience to be fully understood. Advertising on television provides only fleeting information and is usually directed at a single drug; hence the viewer has no means to make a critical or knowledgeable evaluation. The intent of this series of books—*Drugs: The Straight Facts*—is to present to students a readable, intelligent, and accurate description of drugs available for specific diseases, why and how they are used, their limitations, and their side effects. It is our hope that this will provide students with sufficient information to satisfy their immediate needs and give them the background to ask intelligent questions of their health care providers when the need arises.

David J. Triggle, Ph.D.
University Professor
School of Pharmacy and Pharmaceutical Sciences
State University of New York at Buffalo

An in-depth account of drugs and drug discovery can be found in John Mann, *The Elusive Magic Bullet: The Search for the Perfect Drug.* New York: Oxford University Press, 1999.

1

100 Million Women Can't Be Wrong

Every day, in every corner of the world, over 100 million women swallow a small pill. This oral **contraceptive** pill, which contains a large dose of female **hormones**, is the most popular form of birth control among married women in the world, except in India. In the United States, over 80% of all women born after 1945 have used **birth control pills** at some point during their childbearing years as their preferred method of contraception, and it is the most common form of birth control for sexually active unmarried women in sub-Saharan Africa. Approximately 7.6 million women who live in China use the pill, which is the largest national population of birth control pill users according to a 2000 study by the Johns Hopkins University School of Public Health's Population Information Program (Figure 1.1). Nearly one-half of married women in Western Europe were using the pill in 2000, which totaled 60% of all contraceptive users. Today, the United States ranks sixth in the number of pill users (5.6 million), behind China, Germany, Indonesia, Brazil, and Bangladesh. In France, 95% of all women who have been sexually active have used the pill, as opposed to only 4% of Japanese women. The Japanese government only approved the pill in 1999. And in Canada, 7 of 10 pill users over 35 years old have used it for 10 years or more.

Taken regularly, **oral contraceptives** provide the most effective form of birth control. Four decades after the introduction of birth control pills, pharmaceutical companies continue to refine the dosage to enhance both their effectiveness and their safety. Today's

Figure 1.1 The Chinese family-planning and AIDS-prevention experiment that began in November 2004 provided citizens with a card to use in machines that dispense condoms and birth control pills.

low-dose birth control pills are far safer than those used in early years, causing fewer heart, lung, and circulatory complications. They can even be used by a woman during the period of time she is breastfeeding her child. Research continually shows that birth control pills have other therapeutic values as well, providing strong protection against some forms of **ovarian cancer** and helping to treat acne, severe menstrual cramps, endometriosis, irregular **menstrual periods**, and polycystic ovary syndrome (PCOS).

Since the 1980s, doctors have created other ways to deliver female hormones for contraceptive purposes. Hormone patches, vaginal rings, injections of hormones, implanted rods filled with hormones, and even hormone-suffused **intrauterine devices** (IUDs) are becoming more popular. These delivery systems allow women to move from the daily dosing necessary with birth control pills to weekly dosing (**birth control patch**), monthly dosing (**vaginal ring**), three-month dosing (injection), and even multi-year dosing (**implant**). The convenience of less frequent dosing has been shown to increase compliance with a birth control regimen among some women.

A BRIEF HISTORY OF THE BIRTH CONTROL PILL

The idea of using an oral dose of synthetic female hormones to regulate ovulation and prevent conception was first presented in the 1920s. By 1950, scientists had developed relatively inexpensive synthetic female hormones, and after a decade of testing, the United States **Food and Drug Administration (FDA)** approved the first birth control pill in 1960.

The Enovid-10, manufactured by G.D. Searle and Company, contained 9.85 milligrams (mg) of the synthetic progestational hormone norethynodrel and 150 micrograms (1,000 micrograms equals 1 mg) of the estrogenic hormone mestranol. These dosages contain about 10 times the **progestin** and four times the **estrogen** in today's typical low-dose birth control pills.

Early birth control pills had significant side effects, which for many women outweighed the clear benefits of a convenient, reliable, and generally safe way to prevent pregnancy. Among these side effects were headaches, nausea, cramps, irregular menstrual bleeding, breast tenderness, and weight gain. Although these side effects were generally temporary, and did not signify any deeper problems, they were often troublesome enough for women to switch to other, less effective forms of birth control or to stop using birth control altogether.

In addition to the troublesome side effects, oral contraceptives had some real dangers. Epidemiological (population-

Figure 1.2 Some birth control pills come in 28-day dispensers that resemble a makeup compact.

based) research conducted after oral contraceptives were approved showed that the dose of estrogen used in the pill increased the risk of stroke, heart attack, and blood clots in the deep veins of the legs. Although larger and more refined studies showed that these problems occurred far more frequently in women over 35 years old, and especially in women who smoked cigarettes, the media often exaggerated the danger and played down the specifics. This led to several "pill scares" throughout the 1960s and 1970s, which dramatically cut into oral contraceptive use. At the same time, other studies were showing that oral contraceptives had decided benefits against certain forms of cancer, loss of bone density (osteoporosis), and some forms of breast disease.

Today's low-dose birth control pills greatly reduce the side effects and the dangers, without compromising effectiveness (Figure 1.2). Many women still experience side effects during the first few weeks of pill use, but the reduced side effects mean that many more women continue to use oral contraceptives for longer periods of time and gain the benefits of such use. Research has shown that estrogen doses as low as 20 micrograms (mcg) can be 99% effective in preventing pregnancy when combined with the proper progestin dose.

While estrogen doses in all birth control pills currently on the market are less than 50 mcg, with many in the 30 to 40 mcg range, progestin doses vary widely because the different synthetic progestins that have been developed over time vary widely in their potency. The progestin-only pill is a more recent product than the combined progestin-estrogen pill. Progestin-only pills are used by breastfeeding women who want the protection of oral contraceptives without hindering their production of breast milk. Although scientists have determined that estrogen causes many of the unpleasant side effects, few women who are not breastfeeding routinely use progestin-only pills. There are a few reasons for this:

- Progestin-only pills are taken continuously, without any hormone-free days.

- Progestin-estrogen pills are about 99% effective, whereas progestin-only pills are less than 95% effective.

- If a day is missed or if they are not taken at precisely the same time every day, progestin-only pills lose much of their effectiveness.

THE MENSTRUAL CYCLE

The **menstrual cycle** refers to the monthly cycle each woman goes through from the time she reaches puberty in her early teens until the time she reaches menopause, usually in her 40s or 50s. During this cycle, which on average lasts 28 days, the levels of a number of hormones rise to create a hospitable environment for conception and pregnancy to occur, then fall again if conception does not take place.

Each month, an egg (the single cell a female contributes to reproduction) is released from one of the woman's two ovaries—a process known as ovulation—and travels down the **fallopian tube** and into the **uterus**. During the six to seven days it takes to get from the ovary to the uterus, if the egg is met by a sperm (the single cell a male contributes to reproduction), the egg may become fertilized. If a fertilized egg implants in the uterine wall, it may begin to divide and the cells multiply, the first stage of reproduction.

The release of an egg from an ovary occurs about halfway through the menstrual cycle. From the beginning of the cycle until ovulation, levels of a number of female hormones have been rising, causing a host of changes within the woman's reproductive organs. The most important change for the purpose of conception is the thickening of the endometrium (the lining of the uterus), which establishes a welcoming bed of tissue for any fertilized egg to burrow into and begin to nourish itself from the woman's blood flow.

If the egg that has been released from the ovary is not fertilized, it withers in the uterus and is expelled through the **cervix** and out the vagina in a woman's normal flow of secretions (menstruation). The endometrial tissue layer becomes thin again, and the woman begins her menstrual period, during which blood, vaginal and cervical secretions, and endometrial tissue are expelled out the vagina over a period of five to seven days. Immediately after the end of the menstrual period, the hormone levels begin to build again, and about two weeks later another ovulation occurs.

In the United States, most girls have their first menstrual cycle, complete with an episode of menstrual bleeding, some time between their ninth and fifteenth birthday. Typically, girls begin menstruating around age 12 or 13, and it usually takes two to three years until their cycles and menstrual periods become regular and predictable. There are a number of hormones that are important in puberty and in the menstrual cycle. At the beginning of puberty, follicle-stimulating hormone (FSH) and leutinizing hormone (LH) are released from the pituitary gland and travel to the ovaries, where they begin to create follicles (little sacs) around some of the more than 400,000 eggs the typical girl has in her ovaries at that time (at birth, she probably had about 1 million). Once the ovaries become stimulated, they begin to release estrogen, which in turn stimulates the physical changes in body size and shape that occur at puberty.

About two years after the onset of puberty, a girl ovulates for the first time. In the few days leading up to each monthly ovulation, the ovaries secrete increasing amounts of estrogen, which causes the endometrium to grow and thicken. Peak estrogen levels are reached about two days before the actual ovulation occurs, then begin to drop off. At the same time, the follicle that will produce the egg that gets released at ovulation begins releasing small amounts of the hormone progesterone.

The egg that is released from the follicle can be fertilized by a sperm cell at any time once it enters the fallopian tube and before it begins to wither a couple of days after entering the uterus, although it usually occurs in the first day or two of its journey. This means that a teen or woman is most fertile (able to become pregnant) in the early days of the third week of her four-week cycle. This timing is not always perfect, which is why couples who utilize timing methods (often referred to as the rhythm method) for their contraception—timing intercourse only during those days of the month when the women is theoretically least likely to conceive—often end up with unintended (although not necessarily unwanted) pregnancies. And it is why women who are having trouble conceiving often time intercourse with their partners for the days, or even the hours, when they are, according to their meticulous charting of menstrual periods and even body temperature, most likely to conceive. After the follicle has released the egg, the follicle—now known as the corpus luteum—continues to secrete large amounts of progesterone and estrogen. The endometrium continues to thicken and store nutrients to nourish any egg that becomes fertilized and implants.

Girls with certain hormonal imbalances and girls with eating disorders may begin to menstruate later and experience irregular and unpredictable cycles. Reproductive health, including an understanding of a girl's particular menstrual cycle and regularity, are important health issues, and girls should not feel embarrassed to ask questions and seek answers from professionals if they are at all concerned that their menstrual cycles are irregular and unpredictable, or if they feel they are experiencing an unusual level of discomfort or excessive bleeding. These are not uncommon issues, and bringing these concerns to the attention of a health-care provider, at school, at a clinic, or at a doctor's office, is not only appropriate but is to be commended.

THE PILL'S MECHANISM OF ACTION

Birth control pills and all other forms of hormonal contraception have been designed to disrupt this normal hormonal cycle and create an artificial hormonal environment where conception and implantation do not occur (Figure 1.3). Most birth control pills in use today contain a combination of synthetic forms of estrogen and progesterone (progestin). Combined progestin-estrogen birth control pills work in several ways.

- First, the pill blocks the surge of luteinizing hormone (LH) that creates ovulation, meaning that the ovaries do

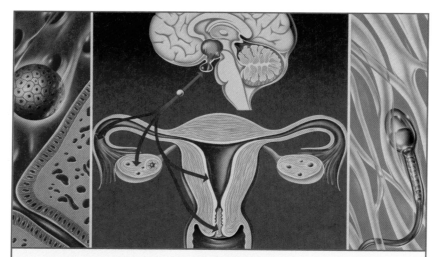

Figure 1.3 Birth control pills cause parts of the brain to stop producing sex hormones. As a result, the release of an egg from the ovaries is prevented (center). In the rare event an egg is released, the lining of the uterus is altered to prevent implantation (left). Other areas of the uterus thicken to block the passage of sperm (right).

not release eggs into the fallopian tubes. Without an egg to fertilize, conception cannot occur. Studies have shown that there is some "breakthrough" ovulation—meaning that occasionally ovulation does take place despite the lack of LH, which occurs more with today's low-dose pills than in the past with higher-dose pills.

- Second, the pill thickens the cervical mucus, making it harder for sperm to enter the uterus and fertilize an egg or to make its way through the uterus to the fallopian tube to fertilize an egg as it travels down the tube.

- Third, the pill inhibits sperm motility—its ability to travel through the fallopian tube. The same effects that reduce sperm motility in the fallopian tube would also reduce motility of any egg that becomes fertilized. This, along with changes to the endometrium caused by hormones, makes it unlikely that any egg that became fertilized would successfully implant in the uterine wall.

In other words, the pill acts to reduce the chance that an egg will be released from the ovary. It also reduces the ability of sperm to travel in the uterus and the fallopian tube to fertilize any egg that might have been released. And it makes the endometrium a less hospitable host for any egg that is not only released but actually fertilized (which is a very rare occurrence). The hormones in birth control pills do not, however, do anything to destroy any fertilized egg by changing the composition of the fertilized egg. Understanding precisely this mechanism of action is very important in understanding the political/religious/ethical controversy that use of the birth control pill causes in some communities and even in some countries.

The contraceptive effect of the combined progestin-estrogen pill is caused by the progestin content. Estrogen is included for controlling the menstrual cycle; estrogen may also enhance progestin's effect on restricting the LH surge and on changing the condition of the endometrium. The clinical significance of these effects of estrogen without progestin has never been studied.

Progestin-only compounds are also used in "emergency contraception" pills (ECPs), such as **Plan B®**, which can be taken up to 48 to 72 hours after unprotected sex to prevent conception. In fact, before the FDA approved emergency contraception in the late 1990s, doctors often prescribed that women who had had unprotected sex take multiple standard birth control pills over a two-day period to flood their system with hormones.

Birth control pills available in the United States contain one of two estrogen compounds, either ethinyl estradiol (EE) or menstranol. Menstranol is metabolized in the bloodstream into EE, and a higher dose of menstranol is required to provide the same level of estrogen as EE. Today, virtually all combined hormonal pills in use in the United States contain EE. EE is also released by the patch and the vaginal ring. Birth control pills generally contain 20 to 50 mcg of estrogen in a daily dose. The patch releases about 20 mcg of estrogen daily, while the ring releases about 15 mcg. Nine different progestin com-

EMERGENCY CONTRACEPTION CONTROVERSY

Despite numerous recommendations by scientific advisory panels, it took years for the FDA to approve emergency contraceptive pills. These are high-dose synthetic hormone contraceptives that can be used within 48 to 72 hours of unprotected sex to prevent pregnancy. Today, most practitioners prefer the emergency contraceptive pill known as Plan B®. It has a high-dose progestin-only formulation that has fewer side effects than other emergency contraceptives.

Some people, however, believe that emergency birth control pills such as Plan B® should be outlawed. Anti-abortion groups argue that when taken after the act of unprotected sex, emergency contraceptive pills act not as an inhibitor of conception but as an inhibitor of a fertilized egg implanting in the uterine wall. This, they argue, makes the pill a chemical abortion rather than a form of contraception and thus should not be marketed at all.

Women's health advocates argue that this is a non-issue. Research has shown that progestin-only emergency contraception does not disrupt any postfertilization events when studied in rats (to do human studies would not be ethically possible). Women's health advocates argue that anti-abortion forces are deliberately lumping together emergency contraceptives and other drugs, including RU-486, a so-called "chemical abortion" compound that is FDA-approved for use within the first trimester of pregnancy to induce contractions and explusion of an embryo.

pounds are available in birth control pills used in the United States, and three other progestins are used in the other combined-hormone delivery systems (patch and ring).

Progestins have different inherent potencies and unique balances between progesterone activity and residual androgenicity. Androgens are male steroid hormones, and because most synthetic progestin compounds derive from androgens, they all contain levels of androgens. One combined-formulation birth control pill available since 2004 contains a new class of compound, drospirenone, which is derived from an antihypertensive compound (one that controls high blood pressure). The dose of progestin in birth control pills varies from 0.15 to 1.0 mg. The patch releases about 150 mcg of the progestin compound norelgestromin into the system every day, and the patch releases about 120 mcg of the progestin compound etongestrel each day.

ADMINISTRATION AND USE

Combined birth control pills, as well as patches and vaginal rings, reside in the second tier of contraceptive effectiveness. They have higher failure rates than implants or injections, as well as intrauterine devices (whether or not suffused with hormone). Effectiveness is measured both in terms of "perfect use" and in terms of "typical use."

If used perfectly, only three of every 1,000 women who use birth control pills can statistically be expected to become pregnant in a year, due to breakthrough ovulation followed by successful **fertilization** and implantation. However, the actual first-year failure rate in a population of typical users is about 8%, meaning that 1 in every 12 women who begin using the pill and remain sexually active can expect to become pregnant in the first year. Why is this?

First, mistakes with taking the pill frequently increase the number of "pill-free days" in any cycle. Most women who use birth control pills use a 28-pill packet that closely follows a woman's standard menstrual cycle. One pill is taken every day. Physicians suggest that the pill be taken at the same time each day to create a routine. The pill should be taken with food or milk, to reduce intestinal upset. It should not be taken at the same time as certain other medications are taken.

A 28-day packet has 21 pills with active ingredients and seven pills with no active ingredients, known as spacer pills,

RU-486

Discussions and debates about Plan B®—also known as the morning after pill—have often become confused, sometimes deliberately so, with discussions about RU-486, a chemical compound that induces miscarriage (natural abortion). RU-486 has long been available in Europe, and was approved for use in the United States by the Food and Drug Administration (FDA) in the late 1990s. As of March 2006, the drug had been used to induce over 560,000 abortions in the United States.

The hope of abortion-rights advocates who lobbied for approval of RU-486 was that it would provide a safe, effective, and more private way for women to terminate unwanted pregnancies. Since the 1980s, when anti-abortion advocates became increasingly aggressive in their legal, public relations, and protest tactics, it has become much more difficult for women in many areas of the country to access surgical abortion providers. This is due to restrictions placed on abortions by the states, as well as by the reduction in those training in obstetrics and gynecology willing to perform the procedure. Much of this reduction is due to the negative pressure put on providers by anti-abortion protestors who rally not only at abortion clinics, but also at the private offices and even homes of doctors who perform abortions. In the 1990s, three abortion providers were even murdered and abortion clinics were bombed.

to keep track of the days until a new pill cycle begins. During these seven days, women should experience a menstrual period. Because there has been no ovulation, and no resultant hormonal cycle, most women experience menstrual periods with less bleeding and less discomfort while taking birth control pills than they did before beginning to use the pill. Birth control pills are, in fact, sometimes prescribed to

RU-486 is a combination of two chemical compounds, mifepristone and misoprostol. Mifepristone is taken for three days, followed by an administration of misoprostol. The two drugs combine to dislodge the fetus from the uterine wall, induce uterine contractions, and expel the fetus. The entire process usually takes 10 to 14 days and is accompanied by cramping, some bleeding, and often even some pain. If the treatment fails, a surgical abortion must be performed. While surgical abortions are much quicker, many women appreciate the privacy of being able to have their primary care or gynecological provider prescribe the medication, without having to go to an abortion clinic. Others feel less conflicted about obtaining an abortion that seems more "natural."

RU-486 is not without political and medical controversy. Even though it can only be used in early-stage pregnancy, antiabortion advocates continue to try to limit its use. And in 2005 and 2006, six deaths from the bacterium *Clostridium sordelli* occurred among women who used RU-486. Four of the six had administered the misoprostol vaginally rather than orally (there is a medical debate about the more effective route of administration for this drug, which is the one that induces the contractions). This incidence of death (6 in 560,000) is far greater than the incidence of deaths from surgical abortions (about 1 in a million in the United States since the 1990s).

women with iron-deficiency **anemia** due to excessive menstrual bleeding.

The 91-day packet, marketed under the name *Seasonale®*, has 84 pills with active ingredients and seven pills with no active ingredients. A woman using this method only has one period every three months, or every change of season; hence the name *Seasonale®*. These birth control pill cycles are used most frequently by women who suffer from anemia because of dysfunctional uterine bleeding in order to minimize the number of menstrual periods per year. However, some women simply want the convenience of fewer menstrual periods each year, continuous contraceptive protection, and ease of use.

Other ways to create extended use cycles include "bicycling," the back-to-back use of two 28-day packs in a row, but not using the seven days of inactive pills in the first pack (42 days on, then seven days off); "tricycling" (combining three sets, using only the inactive pills from the third set) to create 63 days on and seven days off; or continuous use (called "no cycling").

If taken within six days of the start of a menstrual period, or within six days after an abortion or miscarriage, the pill can be effective immediately. If begun at any other time in the menstrual cycle, the pill becomes fully effective after the first 28-day cycle. To make sure the pill is fully effective, most doctors and other practitioners suggest that a second form of contraception be used for the first month after a woman begins using the pill.

As a final precaution, the pill does not guard against sexually transmitted diseases. For any sexually active person, only condoms provide an effective protection against sexually transmitted diseases.

BENEFITS AND RISKS OF BIRTH CONTROL PILLS

When used correctly, birth control pills are highly effective in preventing pregnancy, and, as we'll discuss in the next chapter,

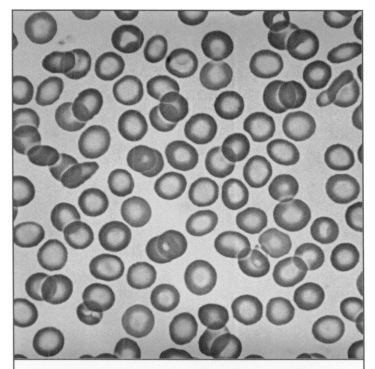

Figure 1.4 A light micrograph shows that this patient suffers from iron-deficiency anemia.

the risks of pregnancy and childbirth—especially for women in less-developed countries and for teenagers—far outweigh the risks of oral contraceptives. Birth control pills regulate and control a woman's menstrual cycle, which provides numerous benefits, especially in reducing iron-deficiency anemia caused by heavy menstrual bleeding. (Figure 1.4). While iron-deficiency anemia is a problem for women all over the world, in less-developed countries women are less likely to receive comprehensive health care, and therefore are less likely to receive treatment for this problem. In industrialized nations, women who experience excessive menstrual bleeding can often replenish the iron lost through dietary changes and the use of iron supplements, but this is not always possible for women in less-developed countries.

Birth control pills also provide protection against some forms of cancer, especially **endometrial cancer** (cancer of the lining of the uterus) and epithelial ovarian cancer. There is also some evidence that birth control pills provide some protection against colon cancer. The use of birth control pills may also provide protection against loss of bone density, development of ovarian cysts, and benign breast disease.

Birth control pills are often prescribed for adolescent girls and young women as a means to regulate menstrual periods. Many adolescents and young women suffer from irregular or absent menstrual periods. Others have a problem called polycystic ovary syndrome (PCOS), a condition caused by a hormonal imbalance. Symptoms include irregular menstrual periods, severe acne, and excess hair growth. Birth control pills are also prescribed for adolescent girls whose ovaries do not produce enough estrogen, either because of anorexia nervosa (an eating disorder), excessive exercise, or the effects of chemotherapy or radiation used earlier to treat a childhood cancer.

Finally, because of their ability to regulate hormonal levels throughout a woman's menstrual cycle, birth control pills have also been shown to relieve both the symptoms of pre-menstrual syndrome (PMS), which include bloating, cramping, pelvic pain, and tender breasts, as well as the symptoms of mittelschmerz syndrome, the mid-cycle pain some women have in conjunction with the ovarian follicle swelling and an egg being extruded from the ovary. Women who use the pill also experience fewer migraine headaches associated with their menstrual periods, and fewer ovarian cysts.

While these health benefits of birth control pills—especially today's low-dose pills—clearly outweigh the risks, use of the pill is not risk free. Women who have a history of heart disease, stroke, or circulatory disorders such as blood clots should not use the pill as their form of contraception. Long-term epi-demiological studies have shown that pill users are somewhat more prone to changes in carbohydrate metabolism—which can be a precursor to diabetes—and have an increased risk of gallbladder disease and noncancerous liver tumors.

DRUG INTERACTIONS

Birth control pills interact with other prescription, over-the-counter (OTC), and street drugs. Some interactions render the birth control pills less effective, which can result in break-through bleeding and/or unplanned pregnancy. Other interac-tions either reduce or increase the effects of the other drugs being taken. This may require a change in dose of either the birth control pill or the other medication.

Before beginning the use of birth control pills, a woman should tell her health-care provider prescribing the pill about all other medication she takes. This includes both prescription as well as OTC medications. In addition, the health-care provider needs to know about any vitamin supplements, herbal supplements, or other natural remedies being used.

Among the drugs that have been shown either by research or through anecdotal evidence to reduce the effectiveness of birth control pills are:

- Anticonvulsive medications (medications that control seizures), such as carbamazepine (Tegretol®), phenobarbi-tal (Luminal®, Solfoton®), and phenytoin (Dilantin®). A woman being treated with anticonvulsives should use a high-estrogen formulation (at least 35 mcg EE) and should also use a barrier method contraceptive (condom or diaphragm) for the first three months of pill use. If no breakthrough bleeding occurs during the three months, she can rely on the pills only after that. Many women who take anticonvulsives need a 50 mcg EE formulation to control breakthrough bleeding. No tests have been conducted on whether or not these medications affect efficacy of patches or rings. A progestin-only injection (**Depo-Provera**®) may be the best option.

- Aspirin and other nonsteroidal anti-inflammatories such as ibuprofen (Motrin® or Advil®) or naproxen (Aleve® or Naprosyn®).

- Oral steroids (used to reduce inflammation) such as prednisone (Deltasone®), prednisolone (Prelone®), or dexamethasone (Decadron®, Dexone®).

- Blood thinners such as warfarin (Coumadin®) or heparin.

- Protease inhibitors used to treat human immunodeficiency virus (HIV), the virus that causes acquired immunodeficiency syndrome (AIDS). Different protease inhibitors either increase or decrease the serum levels of both estrogen and progesterone. A woman who takes protease inhibitors may use birth control pills, but she and her practitioner must take the time necessary to find the formulation that is appropriate for her, given the HIV medication she uses.

- Antibiotics used to treat tuberculosis, such as rifampicin, and even broad-spectrum antibiotics such as ampicillin (Principen®), clarithromycin (Biaxin®), and metronidazole (Flagyl®). While broad-spectrum antibiotics have been shown to decrease the serum levels of both estrogen and progestin, these levels remain within the therapeutic dose, meaning that enough of these hormones are present to maintain the effectiveness of the birth control pill. This is not true for rifampicin, which has been shown to greatly increase the clearance of EE and progestin through the liver. One small study of this interaction has been conducted, and no breakthrough ovulation occurred. However, product labels continue to caution against using birth control pills while using rifampicin.

- Antidepressants, such as fluoxotine (Prozac®).

Physicians recommend that a woman continue using her current birth control pill formulation and add a second form of contraception, such as a condom and spermicide, during the duration of treatment if any of these medications are being taken short-term. If a medication is used for long-term treatment, the birth control pill prescription can be changed to a formulation with at least 50 mcg of estrogen to increase pill effectiveness, or the woman can use another method of contraception. If use of the pill must be stopped for the purpose of short-term treatment with a medication that is made ineffective by the pill, once the treatment ends, pill use can begin again, with a new start-up regimen. That is, if use of the pill started within six days of the beginning of a menstrual period, it is effective immediately; if use is started at any other time in the menstrual cycle, it becomes effective after 30 days of continuous use.

SUMMARY

In the nearly half century that birth control pills have been in use, researchers have continued to refine formulations to make them safer, more effective, easier to use, and less likely to cause unpleasant side effects. Lower-dose formulations provide access to birth control pills to groups of women for whom earlier formulations were unsafe or led to incapacitating side effects. Understanding of the interaction between birth control pills and other beneficial medications has led to the ability to continue birth control pill use for many women being treated for a host of health problems.

At the same time, advances in female hormonal contraceptive technology have led to the ability to deliver the same doses of the hormones found in birth control pills in other forms—such as implants, vaginal rings, suffused intrauterine devices, and skin patches—that provide convenience, ease of use, and longer-term effectiveness, and thus work better than the pill for particular populations of women.

Today, over 100 million women around the world are using birth control pills, and 100 million women can't be wrong.

2

Health Benefits of Birth Control

While pregnancy and childbirth do not normally pose an undue health burden for women in developed countries, this is not the case in Third World nations. Family planning methods, including the birth control pill, not only work to reduce the number of children born but more importantly the number of pregnancies a women has, and the resulting health risks she endures (Figure 2.1).

Reduction in family size has for centuries occurred as societies urbanize and develop economically. While it is necessary to have many children in an agrarian economy—in order to help with farming, caring for livestock, and caring for younger children and elders while parents work to provide food—in societies that produce industrial goods or post-industrial services, the need for large families dissipates. In addition, as societies develop and health care improves, more children live past infancy and childhood, so it is not as necessary to bear many children in order for enough to survive to adulthood to provide for parents as they age.

To this day, in less-developed countries in Asia, Africa, and the Americas, it is not uncommon for women to endure more than a dozen pregnancies, resulting in between 6 and 10 live births, but only have two to four children live beyond the age of five or six. Thousands of children die every week in these countries of bacterial, viral, and parasitic infections that no longer exist in the industrialized world and could easily be treated if the medicines were available. Multiple pregnancies and births put a huge burden on the health of

Study finds risks cut by use of 'the pill'

New findings from the Women's Health Initiative – the largest women's health study ever conducted – found women taking the birth control pill had lower risks of heart disease, stroke and no increased risk of breast cancer, contrary to previous studies.

Health risks lowered due to use of the birth control pill

HEALTH RISK	PERCENT LOWERED	
Heart disease	8%	
High cholesterol	11%	
Chest pains	9%	
Heart attack	10%	
Peripheral artery disease	12%	
Any cancer	7%	13%
Uterine cancer	18%	30%
Ovarian cancer	19%	42%
	IF USED FOUR OR MORE YEARS	

SOURCE: Women's Health Initiative   AP

Figure 2.1 The results of this study on birth control pills and their effect on heart disease and cancer in women show some of the health-promoting effects of birth control pill use.

women in these societies, many of whom have their first pregnancy while still in their early or mid teens.

Many women die during childbirth, and many babies are stillborn because proper nutrition and prenatal health care is lacking. Other women are permanently crippled by recto-vaginal fistulas, which occur when the skin that separates the rectum and the vagina becomes torn during childbirth. This is a frequent problem for younger teens, whose pelvic structure is not always developed enough for a baby to exit the uterus through the vagina, and who often give birth in rural health clinics or at home without proper obstetric care. If these fistulas are not corrected—and they are rarely corrected in less-developed countries—these girls and women may become incontinent (unable to control their flow of urine or feces). The constant dribble of urine and feces can make them susceptible to disease, and the odor can make them outcasts in their communities.

But death, permanent disability, and pregnancy-related difficulties are not only a problem in less-developed countries. In the United States, the **Centers for Disease Control and Prevention (CDC)** estimated that there were approximately 11.8 pregnancy-related deaths per 100,000 live births during the 1990s. The CDC also stated that nearly half the pregnancies in the United States are unplanned. This does not mean they were all technically "unwanted," only that they were not deliberate. Among pregnancy-related risks are ectopic pregnancy, anemia, high blood pressure, infection, maternal death during childbirth, and the development of recto-vaginal fistulas during the birth process.

Pill effectiveness requires correct and consistent use because missed pills and irregular or intermittent use reduce effectiveness. A **World Health Organization (WHO)** study of 15 developing countries in the late 1980s found a pregnancy rate of 6 per 100 users per year, when counselors worked with women to make sure they took their pills regularly. This ratio compares favorably with the 1 or 2 per 100 users per year in industrialized countries and the 3 per 100 users per year among women in less-developed countries who use intrauterine devices (IUDs). Development of long-term hormonal birth control methods such as implants, rings, and patches has increased the effectiveness of hormonal birth control in the developing world.

By preventing ovulation, birth control pills prevent ectopic pregnancies (pregnancies where the fetus implants and begins to develop in the fallopian tube), a potentially life-threatening condition (Figure 2.2). Ectopic pregnancy is more common than generally realized: In the United States, it accounts for as many as one of every 13 emergency room visits by women during the first trimester of pregnancy. Ectopic pregnancy is the

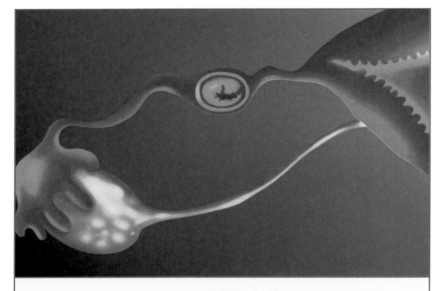

Figure 2.2 An ectopic pregnancy occurs when the fertilized egg does not implant in the uterine cavity, but rather begins to grow in the fallopian tube.

leading cause of pregnancy-related deaths during the first trimester and the second leading cause (about 9%) of pregnancy-related deaths overall.

MENSTRUAL BENEFITS

In addition to reducing the dangers of pregnancy and childbirth, birth control pills provide a number of other health benefits for women around the world. By reducing menstrual bleeding, birth control pills reduce the incidence of iron-deficiency anemia, a common and serious problem for women worldwide, but especially in less-developed countries. Regular and predictable menstrual cycles, and menstrual periods with less bleeding, lead to a better quality of life because women suffer less **dysmenorrhea** (painful menstrual periods) and less severe premenstrual symptoms.

MENSTRUAL DISORDERS AND BIRTH CONTROL PILLS

Women may suffer from a number of menstrual disorders. These are generally considered "nuisance" problems, often uncomfortable but rarely a serious threat to a woman's health.

The most dangerous of these problems is heavy periods (menorrhagia). A heavy menstrual period lasts more than seven days and causes an unusually high amount of bleeding. Heavy periods are most common among young women who are not ovulating regularly and among older women approaching menopause.

Menorrhagia may be caused by a number of underlying conditions: Non-cancerous fibroid tumors in the uterus; a pelvic infection, often caused by a sexually transmitted disease; or endometriosis, a condition where endometrial tissue from the lining of the uterus sloughs off from the uterine wall and lodges in other tissue of the reproductive tract. A one-time event in which a period begins late and involves excessive bleeding is often the sign of a miscarriage.

A gynecologist diagnoses the cause of menorrhagia by conducting a thorough physical examination, including a pelvic exam to check the cervix and uterus. The doctor may also take a Pap smear and tissue biopsies. If the reproductive organs are found to be normal, the cause of the menorrhagia is assumed to be hormonal and treatment with estrogen, progesterone, or both is prescribed. Doctors often use birth control pills for this purpose, especially in teens and younger women with no risk factors that would make them poor candidates for pill use. Birth control pills both regulate the menstrual period and generally lead to less bleeding.

Reduced Menstrual Bleeding

It is generally agreed that 60% to 80% of women who use birth control pills experience less bleeding during their menstrual periods than non-pill users. On average, they lose 50% to 60% as much blood as non-pill users. This reduced blood loss decreases the loss of iron in red blood cells and reduces the severity of iron-deficiency anemia. Birth control pills also reduce the incidence of anemia suffered during pregnancy. Anemia is a serious health problem for women in less-developed countries, due to repeated pregnancies, poor diet, and parasites. Some 28-day birth control pill packets contain spacer pills that include an iron supplement to increase iron levels. Studies in developing countries have found that after one year of birth control pill use, women have higher levels of both hemoglobin (a measure of iron in the red blood cells) and serum iron.

More Regular Menstrual Cycles and Less Discomfort

Studies have shown that the use of birth control pills acts to regulate menstrual cycles, reduce painful menstruation, and reduce pre-menstrual symptoms. In England, a long-term study by the Oxford University Family Planning Association found that pill users or those who had used birth control pills in the previous year were two-thirds as likely to be referred to a hospital for treatment of irregular menstrual periods. Only 7% of pill users reported irregular periods compared to 12% of women who did not use birth control.

About half of all women experience dysmenorrhea (painful menstrual periods) at some time in their lives, and for 10% of women the discomfort interferes with their day-to-day activities. Birth control pills, which generally produce shorter and lighter periods, have become the standard treatment for dysmenorrhea.

Most women report experiencing premenstrual symptoms at some point, and for some women, the symptoms are severe enough to affect daily living. These symptoms, brought on by natural changes in hormone levels, usually begin in the middle of the menstrual cycle, become most severe in the last few days before a menstrual period begins, and subside once the period starts. Among the more common symptoms are pelvic pain, headache, backache, fatigue, breast soreness, bloating, acne, and changes in sexual desire. Severe symptoms include difficulty concentrating, nervousness, anxiety, irritability, and even depression. A woman who regularly suffers from the cluster of severe symptoms is said to have premenstrual syndrome (PMS). Birth control pills have been found in several studies to reduce both the duration and severity of premenstrual symptoms.

DISEASE PROTECTION

Use of the pill also reduces the risk of cancers of the uterine lining and the ovaries. Some evidence suggests that the pill also reduces the risk of colorectal cancer, benign breast disease, ovarian cysts, and loss of bone density. It also improves acne. Birth control pills are thought to protect against these cancers by reducing the rate of cell division in the endometrial tissue of the uterus. They may provide protection against ovarian cancer by reducing gonadotropin (follicle-stimulating hormone) production in the pituitary gland.

Endometrial Cancer

To date, only combined estrogen-progestin birth control pills have been studied for their effects on endometrial cancer. Although no studies have yet been conducted on progestin-only pills, research suggests that it is the progestin that provides protection against the rapid cell division in the endometrial tissue that leads to cancer. Both case-control studies and cohort studies have found that longer use of birth control pills provides increased protection, but that even one year's use provides benefits long after a woman stops using birth control pills. Studies conducted in the United States and Great Britain suggest that one year of birth control pill use reduces the risk of endometrial cancer to 77% of that among nonusers; two years of use reduces the risk to 62%; four years, 49%; eight years, 36%; and 12 years of use reduces the risk to only 30% that of nonusers. This protection lasts as much as 10 years after the end of birth control pill use.

Epithelial Ovarian Cancer

Studies have shown that women who use birth control pills for 10 years or more reduce their risk of epithelial ovarian cancer, the most common cancer of the ovaries, to 20% of nonusers (Figure 2.3). To date, studies have only included women under 55 years old. Most ovarian cancers occur in women over 60 years old, and those women who used birth control pills in the earliest years after the pill's approval by the FDA are just now turning 60. Because evidence shows that the benefits of pill use last long after initial use, over the next 20 years scientists will be able to study many effects of birth control pills on epithelial ovarian cancer they have not yet observed. Most women stop using birth control by age 50, so by age 60, when they reach the age at which most ovarian cancers occur, they have already been off birth control pills for 10 years or more. Widespread use of birth control pills beginning in the 1970s and continuing to this day may result in a noticeable decline in this usually deadly form of cancer in the years to come.

Colorectal Cancer

Colorectal cancer is the fifth most common cancer among women worldwide and is often deadly. Although there is less definitive evidence than that regarding endometrial or ovarian cancers, some case-control studies have shown that women who have used birth control pills reduce their risk of colorectal cancer to 60%, and that use of birth control pills for two years

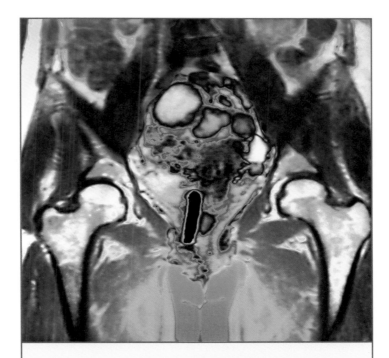

Figure 2.3 This magnetic resonance image of a frontal section through the abdomen of a 28-year-old woman shows ovarian cancer (brown, upper center).

reduced the risk to 50%. However, other studies have shown no benefits of birth control pill use, so research is continuing.

OTHER HEALTH BENEFITS

Preliminary research suggests that use of birth control pills decreases loss of bone density over time and reduces the incidence of ovarian cysts and benign breast disease.

Use of birth control pills may reduce or even prevent bone density loss, and may continue to have beneficial effects even after regular use of the pill ceases and menopause (when ovulation and menstrual cycles end) sets in. A retrospective study of 2,297 women, 76% of whom were postmenopausal, found

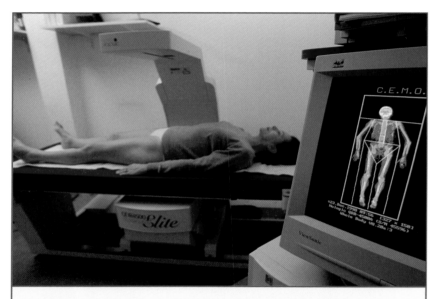

Figure 2.4 A bone densitometer measures the density of bones. The monitor displays readings while the patient lies beneath the machine.

that women with higher bone density were more likely to have used birth control pills during their childbearing years than were women with lower bone density. Other studies have found that use of birth control pills reduced fractures in older women. Clinical studies suggest that estrogen in birth control pills provides the protection against bone-density loss (Figure 2.4).

One area where today's low-dose birth control pills have proven to be less effective than previous high-dose formulations (over 50 mcg of estrogen) is in protection against ovarian cysts. While high-dose birth control pills reduced the risk of many types of ovarian cysts to as little as 20% compared to nonusers, low-hormone formulations provide little to no protection. The same is true for protection against benign breast disease. Higher-dose formulations of birth control pills provided exceptional protection against fibroadenoma and fibrocystic breast disease, reducing the incidence to about 25% compared to nonusers. Studies have shown that protection against benign breast disease is dependent to some extent on the amount of progestin in the formulation, the particular synthetic progestin used, and the length of time birth control pills are taken.

The FDA has approved the use of two birth control pill formulations with high estrogenicity and low androgenicity (Ortho Tri-Cyclen® and Estrostep®) for the treatment of mild to moderate acne in adolescent girls, as well as for treatment of a syndrome called polycystic ovary syndrome (PCOS), the symptoms of which include acne, excess facial and/or body hair, and a tendency to develop ovarian cysts. The pills lower the concentration of male sex hormones (androgens) and increase the concentration of estrogen.

Other potential health benefits of birth control pills include a reduced risk of developing rheumatoid arthritis and, in formulations with higher EE levels and lower androgen levels, a favorable effect on blood lipids (increased HDL cholesterol and reduced LDL cholesterol).

Some manufacturers have added vitamins to their spacer pills, and some are working on ways to add 44 mcg of folic acid to both their active and spacer pills. Folic acid is a B-complex vitamin necessary for a healthy neurological system; too little folic acid during pregnancy has been shown to be a factor in neural-tube birth defects such as spina bifida, where the bottom of the spinal column does not close during gestation.

SUMMARY

Since the 1960s, when birth control pills first became available, scientists and epidemiologists have studied birth control use and the differences in health status of women who use birth control pills and those who don't. In hundreds of studies, birth control pills have been shown to enhance health status on many different levels. However, many studies are not definitive, and many people would argue that the pill's health-enhancing effects on certain diseases are offset by its detrimental effects on other health measures.

But there is little if any argument about the greatest health-enhancing effects of birth control pills. Every study has shown that whatever the increased risks of birth control pills, the risks of pregnancy and childbirth are far greater. This is especially true for teens in industrialized countries and for all women in less-developed countries. It can be said with certainty that, especially in the developing world, birth control pills have saved the lives of millions of women and improved the health status and living standards of tens of millions more.

3

Birth Control Pills and Disease

While today's birth control formulations are far less dangerous than those of the 1960s and 1970s, there is still some evidence that use of birth control pills or other female hormonal contraceptive delivery systems (implants, injections, patches, vaginal rings, or suffused intrauterine devices) does create some health risks. These risks are more likely to be exacerbation of underlying medical conditions than medical problems "caused by" use of hormonal contraceptives. Most of these risks have to do with the circulatory system, including the heart.

CIRCULATORY SYSTEM DISEASES

Major health risks resulting from the use of birth control pills are circulatory diseases, such as heart attack and stroke. These are more common in women over 35 years old, and much more common among women who smoke cigarettes and those who have high blood pressure. Lower-dose birth control pill formulations that have been in use since the 1990s have greatly reduced these risks. Even in countries with a small number of pregnancy-related deaths, the pill is safer than pregnancy and childbirth for all women except those who are over 35 and who smoke cigarettes and/or have high blood pressure.

The large number of women who have used birth control pills since the 1980s, and the number of women who have used them for a long time (more than 10 years), has made it possible to conduct studies of long-term use and to better identify those women likely to experience health problems as a result of birth control pills. The most common health problems in those who use birth control pills are diseases of the circulatory system such as:

- Heart attack

- Stroke

- Deep vein thrombosis (DVT), an obstruction of a blood vessel by a blood clot

- High blood pressure

CASE-CONTROL, COHORT, AND RETROSPECTIVE STUDIES

Scientists who study the effects of disease, pharmaceuticals, or naturally occurring events on people are known as epidemiologists. They generally use one of three methodologies to conduct their studies: the case-control model, the cohort model, or the retrospective model.

In a case-controlled epidemiological study, public health investigators compare the experiences of a group of people who have experienced a particular circumstance (such as illness, drug intake, or presence at an event) with a comparable group of people who have not encountered the same circumstance. In a case-control study, usually two control patients are examined for every case patient. Control patients are those who have not experienced the circumstance being studied and case patients are those who have encountered the circumstance. Case-control studies are frequently used in studies of an infectious disease in a specific population to pinpoint the source of an outbreak.

Evidence that any use of birth control pills increased the risk of developing these circulatory problems first came to light in the 1970s. However, more recent studies involving current lower-dose formulations of birth control pills have consistently shown that the risks are minimal for women under 35 years old who do not smoke and/or have underlying high blood pressure. Smoking and high blood pressure are two of the greatest risks for heart attack and stroke for anyone in the population, along with a family history of heart attack and a sedentary lifestyle.

Heart Attack

Myocardial infarction (a heart attack) is an event that causes the death of heart muscle cells. A heart attack is brought on by

A cohort study, also known as a prospective study, examines only those people who encounter a particular circumstance. The study does not make any comparisons to people who do not encounter the circumstance. Cohort studies seek to answer the question, "How many people who have a certain experience later have another identical experience?" For instance, a cohort study might seek to answer the question, "How many troops who serve in Iraq will later develop post-traumatic stress disorder?" Such a study would track enough returning service personnel to be statistically significant, over a long enough time, to capture those cases of post-traumatic stress disorder (PTSD) that do not surface until after the service experience.

Retrospective studies seek to make a connection between the onset and cause of a condition or phenomenon. A retrospective study of bone density among post-menopausal women might seek to find a relationship between older women with normal bone density and a prior phenomenon, such as use of birth control pills.

ischemic heart disease, a blockage in circulation that causes the heart to be deprived of adequate blood supply. This blockage can be brought on by atherosclerosis, a long-term development of deposits on the blood vessel walls that reduce the flow of blood. Or it can be brought on suddenly by a thrombus, a blood clot that blocks the blood flow.

Myocardial infarction is a rare occurrence in young women, but it is less rare in young women who smoke. Early studies involving high-dose birth control pills showed a risk in pill users of two to four times that of nonusers. More recent studies involving lower-dose formulations have shown the users' risk to be less than two times that of nonusers. Third-generation pills have been shown not to increase the risk of heart attack at all over the risk among women who have never used birth control pills.

Recent case-control studies show an estimated 5% of myocardial infarctions among women to be the result of pill use. This equals approximately three additional heart attacks per one million per year among those women who use the pill. Other case-control studies conducted in the United States and Great Britain have shown nearly identical risks among users and nonusers. The World Health Organization (WHO) has conducted the largest multi-center study of relationships between pill users and circulatory diseases. The WHO found that in both developed and less-developed countries, when women are checked for high blood pressure before beginning use of the pill and the pill is not offered to women with high blood pressure, there is virtually no additional risk of heart attack.

All studies have shown that heart attack risk does not increase the longer a woman uses birth control pills. In addition, any additional risk created by use of the pill disappears once use is discontinued.

Stroke

The term *stroke* refers to an event that leads to the death of brain cells. There are two causes of stroke: the disruption of blood flow to the brain, called an ischemic stroke, or a blood vessel in the brain rupturing, called a hemorrhagic stroke. Young women who have a stroke most frequently suffer from a subarachnoid hemorrhagic stroke, in which blood from the ruptured blood vessel floods the space below the brain's arachnoid membrane.

Early studies of pill users in the 1960s and 1970s suggested that women who used birth control pills were more than five times more likely to suffer any form of stroke than nonusers. More recent studies involving women taking lower-dose formulations of birth control pills suggest that there is far less risk. These studies have provided far better data regarding ischemic stroke than hemorrhagic stroke.

A WHO study—the largest case-control study of stroke among pill users—determined that, as with heart attack, other risk factors make a significant difference in the relationship between stroke and the use of birth control pills. Those who use birth control pills and do not have high blood pressure are only 1.5 times more likely to suffer an ischemic stroke than nonusers. Women living in developing countries who smoke and use the pill face approximately two times the risk of those who use the pill but do not smoke (Figure 3.1). In Europe, those who smoke and use the pill are 3.5 times more likely to suffer a stroke than pill users who do not smoke.

Women who take the pill and have high blood pressure, whether or not they smoke, face the greatest risk. In developing countries, these women are five times more likely to have a stroke than pill users who do not have hypertension, and in Europe they are four times more likely. As is the case with heart attacks, women who report having their blood pressure checked before starting the pill have a much lower risk of ischemic stroke than those who do not have their blood pressure checked. Also, risk does not increase with the length of time a woman uses the pill, and any additional risk disappears when a woman discontinues the pill.

Figure 3.1 The combination of birth control pills and smoking may increase the risk of stroke in women. Women interested in using birth control pills should discuss all possible risks with their health-care provider.

Older women who use birth control pills are more likely to suffer a stroke than younger women. According to a WHO analysis, fewer than 20 deaths a year from stroke or heart attack can be attributed to use of the pill among one million users of the birth control pill under 35 years old. For women over 35 years old, between 24 and 96 deaths per year can be attributed to use of the pill, depending on the region of the world.

Migraine headaches have long been linked with ischemic stroke (Figure 3.2). Studies have shown that women with a history of migraine headaches who use birth control pills increase their risk of a stroke two to four times above that of women who suffer from migraines but do not use birth control pills. Women who have severe migraines, with "focal neurological symptoms" such as blurred vision, temporary loss of vision, seeing flashing lights, or having trouble speaking, are at an increased risk of stroke, whether or not they use birth control pills.

The WHO, which has conducted the most thorough research into the relationship among migraines, birth control pills, and stroke, has recommended that women who suffer from migraines with focal neurological symptoms not use the pill. Because of the evidence that hypertension (high blood pressure)—**systolic** pressure over 140 millimeters of mercury (mm Hg) or **diastolic** pressure over 90 mm Hg—combined with use of birth control pills increases the risk of stroke, the WHO has also recommended that women with diagnosed hypertension should be counseled to choose another method of birth control (Figure 3.3). Blood pressure must be checked using proper technique and the diagnosis can only be made after a number of confirming measurements, not on the basis of one reading.

However, in many less-developed countries, it is impractical for women to have their blood pressure taken regularly due to the lack of available health-care services. Even if women were diagnosed with high blood pressure, treating hypertension in these areas of the world is often impractical and rarely a major concern, given other heath-care crises such as AIDS and diarrheal diseases. These areas also tend to be where women's death rates from pregnancy and childbearing are highest.

A WHO analysis concluded that screening but not treating high blood pressure in less-developed countries would, at best, prevent only about 10% of the "excess" strokes and heart attacks attributable to the use of birth control pills. Screening women under 35 years old who do not have other risk factors would be practically meaningless. And there would also be the **"false positive"** diagnoses of high blood pressure that would prevent many women from taking birth control pills who should be taking them. The number of deaths attributable to women who should not be using birth control pills because of

Figure 3.2 Some women who use birth control pills or other hormonal contraceptives suffer from headaches, especially in the first few months after beginning pill use. Headaches can often be alleviated by adjusting the dose or switching to a pill with a different formulation.

high blood pressure are fewer than excess deaths due to pregnancy and childbirth without access to birth control pills.

Deep Vein Thrombosis (DVT)

Thromboembolism refers to a blood clot that obstructs a blood vessel. The most common form of thromboembolism is known as a venous thromboembolism or **deep vein thrombosis (DVT)**. DVTs form in the deep veins of the legs, causing pain

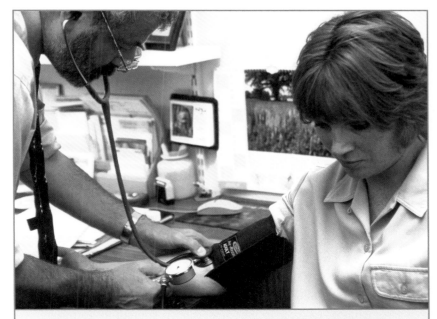

Figure 3.3 Birth control pill use occasionally causes an increase in blood pressure. This can usually be alleviated by adjusting the dose or switching to a different formulation.

(Figure 3.4). One way to prevent DVTs is to avoid staying seated for a long period of time or to not sit in seats that put too much pressure on the legs. People who often travel by air are susceptible to DVTs because of the long periods of time seated, the shape of airline seats, and the tendency to become dehydrated in pressurized airplane cabins. A DVT can break off and travel to the lungs, where it becomes a pulmonary embolism. Pulmonary embolism can be fatal, although it is not common.

Studies of first-generation birth control pills showed a marked increase in risk of developing a DVT—about 80 cases of DVT per 100,000 women who used the pill. However, studies of today's low-dose birth control pills show the risk is not much greater than for nonusers—between 6 and 24 cases of

DVT per 100,000 women, depending on the particular pill formulation. By comparison, about 60 cases of DVT per 100,000 women are associated with pregnancy. Worldwide, among women who do not use birth control pills, an estimated 0.6 to 1.2 deaths per one million women are attributable to DVTs. Case-control studies of pill users suggest that pill use contributes to an additional 1.3 to 2.4 deaths per one million women.

High Blood Pressure (Hypertension)

Studies have shown small but statistically significant increases in blood pressure in women who use birth control pills that contain more than 50 mcg of estrogen. These increases have averaged about 6 mm Hg for systolic pressure and about 2 mm Hg for diastolic pressure. These increases occur regardless of the particular formulation of birth control pill used. For some women, this increase in blood pressure is enough to lead to a diagnosis of hypertension (140/90 mm Hg or higher). Despite the increase, blood pressure remains within normal range for most women.

However, studies show that women in the United States who use birth control pills are about twice as likely to develop high blood pressure over time. The risk of developing high blood pressure increases with the duration of pill use. Once the pill is no longer used, blood pressure generally decreases quickly to the level it was before the woman started taking the pill.

OTHER HEALTH RISKS OF BIRTH CONTROL PILLS

Research has shown that birth control pills affect carbohydrate metabolism, both raising blood sugar levels and decreasing the body's ability to utilize **insulin**. This means that women with diabetes mellitus must be careful about using this form of contraception. Birth control pills have also been associated with an increased risk of gallbladder disease and non-cancerous liver tumors.

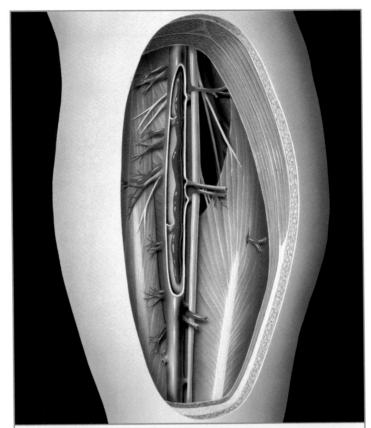

Figure 3.4 Deep vein thrombosis (DVT) can be life threatening. Research shows that use of birth control pills may slightly increase a woman's risk of developing DVT.

Carbohydrate Metabolism

Combined estrogen-progestin birth control pills affect carbohydrate metabolism in two ways that tend to counteract each other. The estrogen increases blood glucose (blood sugar) levels and reduces the ability of insulin, a naturally occurring hormone, to regulate blood sugar. Research shows a direct link between dose and effect: higher doses of estrogen have a greater effect than lower doses. Scientists also believe that the progestin in birth control pills stimulates overproduction of insulin. Diabetes mellitus is the inability of the body to utilize insulin properly, or the inability to make enough insulin to regulate the body's blood sugar level (Figure 3.5).

Despite the effects of birth control pills on blood sugar and insulin production, studies show that users of today's low-dose birth control pills whose initial blood sugar level is within normal range generally maintain a normal level. Scientists believe these women face no increased risk of developing diabetes due to their use of birth control pills. While this is an important finding, the more important question is whether women who are already diabetic can safely use birth control pills. Health-care providers believe that some can, depending on the severity of their diabetes.

Women who are insulin dependent (meaning they inject themselves with synthetic insulin regularly to maintain their blood sugar level) generally see their insulin requirement increase while using birth control pills. However, they are usually able to use birth control pills successfully and for a long time. Women who have diabetes and also suffer from vascular disease, or women who have had diabetes for over 20 years and are therefore at greater risk for developing vascular disease, should not use birth control pills as their family planning method. Women with a history of developing diabetes during pregnancy (known as gestational diabetes) and whose diabetes has self-corrected after the birth of their child or children can safely use birth control pills.

Gallbladder Disease

Current research shows that birth control pills do not cause gallbladder disease. However, in women who are already predisposed to develop **gallstones**, use of birth control pills may speed up the process of forming gallstones. The type of gallstones associated with birth control pills is caused by abnormally high levels of cholesterol in **bile**. Estrogen is thought to

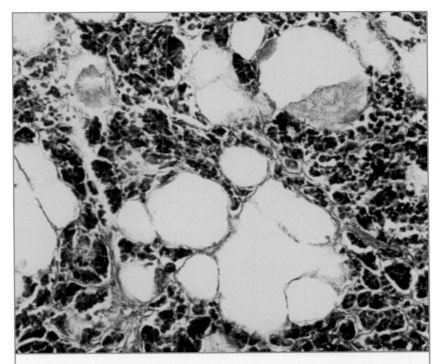

Figure 3.5 This light micrograph shows the pancreas of a person with diabetes. The white spaces indicate a breakdown of the cells that are responsible for producing insulin.

induce high saturation of cholesterol. However, if the user is not predisposed to developing gallstones, the changes in cholesterol level should not cause any outward symptoms.

Liver Tumors

Studies of early, high-dose pill users in the 1970s showed an increase in the development of non-cancerous liver tumors (hepatocellular adenomas). Hepatocellular adenomas are rare, but can be fatal if not treated promptly. These studies showed that incidence of these tumors increased with higher doses of estrogen and with increased time during which the pill was used. In general, the increased incidence of hepatocellular adenomas due to use of the pill was estimated to be three per 100,000 users per year. No thorough studies have been undertaken on the subject with today's low-dose birth control pills, although some evidence has shown up in studies looking at liver cancer.

A number of other health issues regarding birth control pill use have been studied, usually when a person taking birth control pills displays symptoms of a certain condition and researchers look for a causal link.

- Cholestatic jaundice: High-dose birth control pills can impede the transport of bile, leading to this condition. A change in formulation can often reverse the symptoms. If not, birth control pills may have to be discontinued.

- Melanoma: There is no evidence that birth control pills increase the incidence of melanoma, a form of skin cancer. However, doctors recommend that any woman treated for melanoma not get pregnant or use hormonal contraceptives during the three years after treatment when recurrence is most likely to occur.

4

Unresolved Health Issues

Despite their nearly 50-year history of safe and effective use by most women, birth control pills are still associated with some unresolved health issues. These include the relationship between pill use and reproductive tract infections, cervical cancer, breast cancer, and liver cancer.

REPRODUCTIVE TRACT INFECTIONS

Whether or not women who use birth control pills suffer from reproductive tract infections more frequently than women who do not is a complex issue. To date, there is little evidence that any component of birth control pills causes a general increase in reproductive tract infections. There is a possibility that the hormones in the pill lead to cellular changes that enable chlamydia to occur.

The increased rate of infection with chlamydia and other sexually transmitted diseases (STDs) among women who use birth control pills is generally thought to be caused by behavioral differences. In self-reported studies about women's sexual behavior, women who use birth control pills are generally found to have more sexual partners than women who use other means of birth control, to have more frequent intercourse, and to use condoms less frequently. Condoms have been shown to reduce the rate of all sexually transmitted diseases.

CHLAMYDIA AND CHLAMYDIAL PELVIC INFLAMMATORY DISEASE

Most studies show that women who use birth control pills have a higher rate of chlamydia infection than women who use other birth control methods. However, women who use the pill have lower rates of chlamydial pelvic inflammatory disease (PID). Chlamydia is easily treated, but untreated PID is one of the major causes of infertility among women.

Early studies suggested that the increased risk of chlamydia infection among women who use birth control pills was two to three times that of women who do not use the pill. However, more recent and more methodologically sound studies show the risk is about a 70% increase. Some studies show even less increased risk.

This seeming contradiction supports the thesis that higher STD infection rates are caused by differences in behavior. It is also possible that the increase is caused by a higher rate of cervical ectopy found among pill users. Cervical ectopy is a change in the structure of cervical cells—columnar epithelial cells that exist in the cervical canal extend to the vaginal surface of the cervix. Cervical ectopy is thought to create a situation in which this abundance of columnar epithelial cells becomes a target for the *Chlamydia trachomatis* bacteria that cause chlamydia (Figure 4.1). Researchers do not know what, if any, mechanism of action within birth control pills leads to the increase in cervical ectopy. Cervical ectopy may, indeed, be an outcome of chlamydia infection rather than an enabler of infection.

It is also possible that the synthetic hormones in birth control pills may have a positive effect on chlamydial infection. Birth control pills seem to reduce the chances that a woman infected with chlamydia will develop PID, which can happen if the infection moves from the cervix into the fallopian tubes. This reduction in chlamydia becoming PID may be caused by milder uterine contractions during menstruation,

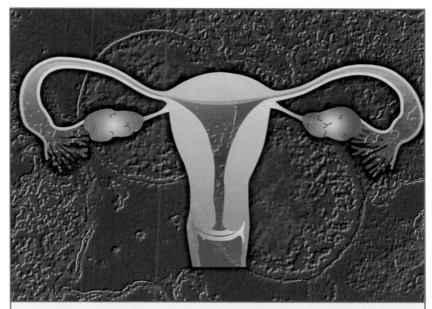

Figure 4.1 Above is an artist's depiction of the female reproductive system superimposed over a micrograph of *Chlamydia trachomatis* bacteria. Most studies show that women who use birth control pills have an increased risk of chlamydia infection.

by less penetrability of cervical mucus because of thickening, or by changes in the woman's immune system. Because studies have included only women hospitalized for PID, and because most PID is not cause for hospitalization, these results are not conclusive. Because other delivery systems for female hormonal contraception have not been in place long enough for long-term research to be done, it is not clear if the same results will occur in users of vaginal rings, suffused intrauterine devices, patches, injections, or implants.

HUMAN IMMUNODEFICIENCY VIRUS (HIV)

There is no conclusive evidence that use of birth control pills increases the risk of contracting the human immunodeficiency

STD RISK AND PREVENTION

STDs are a common problem for American teens who are sexually active. In studies of self-reported sexual activity, 47% of U.S. high school students say that they have had sexual intercourse. Each year in the United States, about 900,000 girls and young women under 20 years old become pregnant (about 340,000 are 17 years or younger). Thirty-five percent of U.S. women have been pregnant at least once before their 20th birthday.

Rates of STDs —syphilis, gonorrhea, chlamydia, HIV, and genital herpes—are higher for U.S. teens than they are for adults. In 2002, infections with chlamydia—a major cause of pelvic inflammatory disease (PID) and its potential for infertility later in life—were six times higher for teenage girls than for adult women.

Chlamydia is caused by the bacterium *Chlamydia trachomatis*, spread from the cervical secretions in women and from the urethral and seminal secretions in men. Women who develop this infection during pregnancy often pass it on to their children, who do not know that they have the infection. Chlamydia is one of the leading causes of blindness in the less-developed world, especially among children, who may inadvertently touch their eyes after touching their genitals, thereby transporting the bacteria. If an individual discovers that he or she has chlamydia, all recent sexual partners must be treated with antibiotics.

Birth control pills do not have any value in protecting against sexually transmitted diseases. The best ways to prevent infection with an STD are, in order of effectiveness:

- Maintaining sexual abstinence
- Being in a monogamous relationship with a person known to be free of STDs
- Using condoms, which are generally (but not completely) effective against the spread of STDs

virus (HIV), which causes acquired immunodeficiency syndrome (AIDS). Studies have consistently shown that among women who use birth control pills there is an increased incidence of HIV infection. Whether the infection occurred before the woman began using the pill or the other way around is difficult, if not impossible, to determine in most cases.

Researchers who have analyzed studies of HIV and birth control pill use have concluded that by using 8 out of 28 studies that are methodologically most sound an increase in risk of about 60% in contracting HIV can be attributed to using birth control pills. Again, it appears that no component of the pill makes a woman more susceptible to becoming infected with HIV. Rather, differences in infection rates can be attributed to differences in behavior—more sexual partners, more frequent intercourse, and less use of condoms.

Use of birth control pills has also been shown to increase the risk of infection with gonorrhea (another sexually transmitted disease) by about 80%. In terms of infections of the reproductive tract that are not sexually transmitted, there is some evidence that use of birth control pills increases the risk of candidiasis, a common yeast infection. And there is conflicting evidence about the relationship between birth control pills and non-sexually transmitted bacterial infections such as *Trichomonas vaginalis*, one of the most common causes of vaginitis (inflammation of the vagina) and the discomfort that comes with it.

CERVICAL CANCER

Most cervical cancers are caused by the human papillomavirus (HPV), a sexually transmitted disease. HPV is common, does not have outward symptoms like warts, and is easily transmitted. Use of a condom—and possibly also use of a diaphragm and spermicide—can reduce the transmission of HPV but cannot eliminate it. The virus lives on areas surrounding the genitals and the anus and can be transmitted without penetration (Figure 4.2).

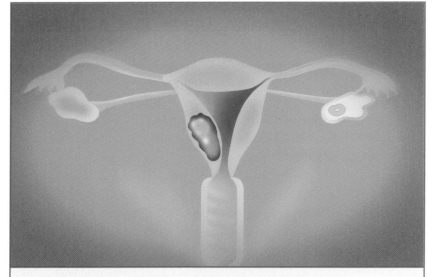

Figure 4.2 A uterine body tumor is located on the cervix. Uterine cancer effects the cervix and the epithelium and can be caused by herpes and papilloma virus infections.

Early engagement in sexual intercourse has also been shown to increase susceptibility to HPV, and therefore an increased risk of developing cervical cancer. Cervical cancer is the final stage of a long process, because this form of cancer has a long "pre-invasive" period. Most pre-invasive lesions do not progress to cervical cancer—they either stop progressing or they actually regress back to the original normal state. Studies have found an increased association between use of birth control pills and both pre-invasive cervical lesions and invasive cervical cancer. It is very difficult to determine if this increased association can be translated into an increased risk. No firm data has shown a higher rate of progression to cancer from pre-invasive lesions among women who use birth control pills.

A number of theories have been proposed about the biological mechanism that would cause women who use birth

Figure 4.3 This technician is analyzing a Pap smear to detect abnormalities, such as cervical cancer.

control pills to develop pre-invasive lesions and/or cervical cancer at a higher rate, although none has been proved. Birth control pills may:

- Change the cervical mucus in a way that increases the risk of being infected with HPV

- Alter a woman's immune system and make her more likely to become infected with HPV

- Produce a deficiency of folic acid in the cervix, which might stimulate the development of pre-invasive lesions

- Speed the rate at which pre-invasive lesions change to become invasive cervical cancers

- Promote cervical ectopy, which in turn promotes infection with HPV

Another possibility for the increased association may be what scientists call detection bias. Especially in less-developed countries, women who use birth control pills usually receive more comprehensive health care than women who use other forms of birth control or none at all. Part of this comprehensive care includes a regular Papanicolaou (Pap) smear to detect changes in cervical cells (Figure 4.3). Other women may have less frequent Pap smears or may not ever have the procedure performed. This means that pre-invasive lesions and cervical cancers may be found in women who use the pill more than in other women simply because they are examined frequently and more thoroughly.

HPV, CANCER, AND A VACCINE

The human papillomavirus (HPV) is an endemic (always present) virus that can cause cervical cancer, one of the most deadly cancers of women. HPV is spread through sexual contact. Scientists believe that, by the age of 30, over 60% of women have been infected with HPV. Most women have built up some level of immunity to the virus, and the vast majority of infections are subclinical, meaning that there are no outward symptoms of the disease. For women who do develop symptomatic HPV, most know they are infected because of the formation of genital warts. Birth control pills and other forms of female hormonal contraception do not guard against the transmission of HPV. Condoms are highly effective against HPV transmission, but not perfect.

Pap smears can be used to test for cell abnormalities in cervical tissue and for the presence of subtypes of HPV that are known to cause cervical cancer. In addition, researchers have developed a vaccine that, when administered to both males and females before their first experience of sexual intercourse, can prevent infection with and spread of HPV. The

BREAST CANCER

The relationship, if any, between use of birth control pills and breast cancer has been debated since the 1970s. In 1996, an organization called the Collaborative Group on Hormonal Factors in Breast Cancer analyzed 54 studies conducted over a 20-year period in 25 countries, both in industrialized and less-developed nations. The aggregate evidence from these studies showed that the incidence of breast cancer among women who have used birth control pills in the past is slightly higher than for women who have never used them. Among the most important findings were:

vaccine was approved by the Food and Drug Administration on June 8, 2006, for use in girls and women between the ages of 9 and 26. Children would be vaccinated at a time that is appropriate for each, given his or her sexual and social development and informed discussion between the child's parents and a health-care provider.

Like many issues involving sexual and reproductive health, the HPV vaccine became a political hot button in the United States. Voices from the socially conservative end of the political spectrum argued that vaccinating children against a sexually transmitted disease is morally wrong and sends a message that adolescent sex is appropriate. The American Academy of Pediatrics (AAP) came out in favor of the vaccination, finding through surveys that only a small minority of its members (about 11%) agree with the socially conservative view. While many pediatricians said in the AAP survey that they feared most parents would balk at a vaccine against a sexually transmitted disease, other surveys have found that parents overwhelmingly follow their pediatrician's advice to vaccinate their children.

1. Current birth control pill users had a 24% higher risk of being diagnosed with breast cancer than did women who had never used the pill. Women who had used the pill and stopped using it within four years of the study had a 16% higher chance of being diagnosed. Women who had stopped using the pill 5 to 10 years before the study were 9% more likely to be diagnosed than those who had never used the pill. For women who had stopped using the pill more than 10 years earlier, there was no increased risk of being diagnosed with breast cancer.

2. The excess risk of diagnosis dealt only with localized breast cancer. Birth control pill users actually had less risk of being diagnosed with cancer that had spread beyond the breast tissue.

3. Women with a family history of breast cancer had no increased risk of diagnosis beyond any risk associated with whether they were then using birth control pills or had stopped using them in the previous 10 years.

4. There was no evidence that the dose of either estrogen or progestin in the birth control pill formulation used was related to an increased risk of being diagnosed with breast cancer.

Scientists who conducted this epidemiological evaluation suggest two possible explanations. One is that use of birth control pills promotes the growth of a tumor that is already present. The second is detection bias—that is, women who use birth control pills generally have more comprehensive health care than women who do not. Good health care and self-care may explain the contradiction that women who use birth control pills are more frequently diagnosed with localized tumors and less frequently diagnosed with breast cancer that has spread (Figure 4.4).

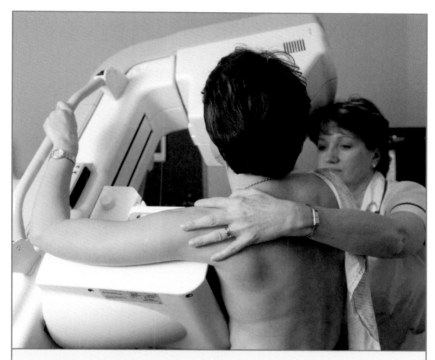

Figure 4.4 This patient is undergoing a mammogram, which is an x-ray of the breast to detect breast cancer or other abnormalities.

LIVER CANCER

Liver cancer is rare and almost always fatal within one year of diagnosis. Some studies have shown that among women who use birth control pills there is an increased risk for developing an extremely rare form of liver cancer, hepatocellular carcinoma. Studies have reported an increased risk of from 2 to 20 times among women who use birth control pills. However, other studies have shown no increased risk at all. Experts suggest that because there has been only a slight increase in death from liver cancer since the 1960s in countries with a high rate of use of birth control pills, such as Sweden and the United States, this connection may be exaggerated.

SUMMARY

It is difficult to concretely attribute the health risks discussed in this chapter to birth control pill use. There are simply too many confounding factors. And it may be that focusing on this particular area changes the results. In the area of human health that is possibly the most private—sexuality and reproduction—the fact that certain women's behavior and health status is closely observed may in fact alter the results of the observation from what they would be in a truly random sample of sexually active women. Women who take part in studies of sexual behavior and reproductive health are, by definition, "self selectors" who agree to allow researchers to probe into their most intimate relationships and medical history. Because of this, it is almost certainly a misinterpretation to say that birth control pill use "causes" changes in health status. Rather, it should be stated that birth control pill use "is associated with" these particular changes in health status. This is a notable difference, especially in an atmosphere where research data is increasingly used to make political and social arguments.

Regardless of any of these risks, use of birth control pills (or other female hormonal delivery methods) is safer for most women, and certainly for teens in industrialized countries and for all women in developing countries, than the risks associated with pregnancy and childbirth.

5

Other Hormonal Contraceptives

Today, the hormones contained in birth control pills can be delivered by other methods for women who would rather not have to remember to take a pill every day. There are five ways to deliver the hormones:

- Injection

- Patch

- Vaginal ring

- Intrauterine devices (IUDs)

- Implantation

Injections, IUDs, and implants use progestin-only formulations. Patches and vaginal rings use combined estrogen-progestin compounds. All of these methods, just like birth control pills, are effective in preventing pregnancy (fewer than 1 pregnancy per 100 women who use the method per year) but do not provide any protection against sexually transmitted diseases.

INJECTION

Depo-Provera® is an injectable form of hormonal contraception. It acts to suppress ovulation and is extremely effective. Research has shown that among perfect users, the chances of becoming pregnant are 0.3 % (3 in 1,000).

Injections are given every three months (12-week cycles), although if a shot is late, most studies have shown Depo-Provera® to be effective for up to 15 weeks. Most women who use this method stop having menstrual periods during the time that they are using Depo injections, but many have some spotting (small amounts of bleeding) for the first three to six months. Women resume their regular cycles 6 to 18 months after they stop using Depo, meaning that a woman using this method must be patient if she stops using Depo with a plan to conceive.

Studies of actual use have found that between 26% and 53% of women who begin using Depo-Provera® continue using it for more than one year. Other studies have shown that intensive counseling at the time of each injection improves continuation rates. Depo-Provera® is more costly than birth control pills and entails a visit to a clinician every three months for a shot, as well as routine laboratory tests. These costs, and the time and inconvenience of added office visits, often outweigh the convenience of not having to take a pill every day, especially for low-income women with limited access to health-care facilities and who often have to use public transportation to get to appointments.

Many women find that they gain weight with Depo. There is also research suggesting that women who use Depo for many years may develop a significant loss of bone density (weak bones), which can be a problem later in life. Depo injections contain only a synthetic progestin (medroxyprogesterone acetate) and can be used by women who can't use estrogen-based hormonal birth control methods. Like all progestin-only formulations, Depo-Provera® has the advantages of no menstrual bleeding and therefore no menstrual-period symptoms or risks from blood loss, low risk of ectopic pregnancy, and no estrogen, which can cause rare but often serious complications including blood clots.

Depo-Provera® has additional advantages. First, it is culturally acceptable where other forms of female hormonal or other types of contraception may not be. In some cultures, a woman may feel more comfortable receiving a medication by injection than by oral pill. In male-dominant cultures, a woman can receive a Depo-Provera® shot without her partner's knowledge,

DEVELOPMENTS IN BIRTH CONTROL TECHNOLOGY

Birth control technology falls into three general categories: surgical, barrier, and hormonal. Male surgery is called a vasectomy, where the tube that carries seminal fluid, including sperm cells, from the testes to the urethra is severed. Vasectomy was originally irreversible, although newer techniques allow the surgery to be reversed if later desired. Female surgery is called tubal ligation, where the fallopian tubes that carry eggs from the ovaries to the uterus are severed and tied. This surgery is irreversible.

The most commonly used barrier methods are the condom, which is worn over the penis to collect semen, and the diaphragm, which is worn inside the vagina to keep semen from passing through the cervix into the uterus. Newer barrier methods include the vaginal sponge and the cervical cap, both worn inside the vagina. The advantages of these methods are that they can be worn effectively for a longer period of time than a diaphragm.

Hormonal contraceptives continue to focus on changing the female cycle. Refinement of birth control pills continues to make them safer, while other hormonal methods (injections, patches, implants, IUDs, and vaginal rings) are designed to make hormonal birth control easier and longer-lasting than daily pills. Scientists are now developing male hormonal birth control methods. Also, researchers are experimenting with using a nasal spray to deliver hormones to both men and women, although this technology may not happen until far into the future.

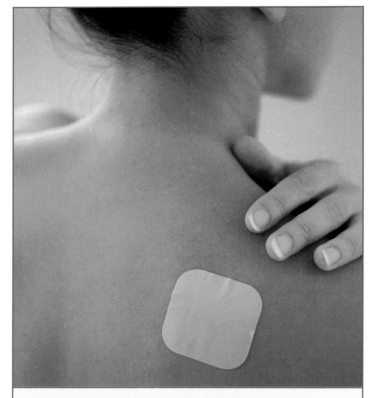

Figure 5.1 This woman wears a contraceptive patch attached to her shoulder. The patch continuously supplies progestin and estrogen hormones to the bloodstream through the skin, to prevent pregnancy.

unlike having pills around the home or putting in a diaphragm before intercourse.

Depo-Provera® also has been shown to have few drug interactions. Its use has been associated with a decrease in the frequency of grand mal seizures, and some studies suggest a causal effect, probably due to the sedative effect of progestins. Women who suffer from sickle cell anemia or sickle cell disease have fewer crises when they use Depo-Provera® than other hormonal contraceptives.

Unfavorably, Depo-Provera® has been shown to adversely affect lipids—an increase in low-density lipoproteins (LDL or bad cholesterol) and a decrease in high-density lipoproteins (HDL or good cholesterol)—and to decrease bone density in long-term users. Also, although rare, some women have had severe allergic reactions to Depo-Provera®.

PATCH

Ortho-Evra® delivers hormones into the bloodstream through a patch that is worn on the skin, similar to the nicotine patches used by people who are trying to quit smoking. The patch is about 2 × 2 inches and looks like a square bandage (Figure 5.1). The patch has three layers—a protective outer layer, a medicated adhesive inner layer, and a clear layer that is removed from the medicated layer before the patch is applied.

The patch is placed on the skin at the beginning of each week for a three-week period. A menstrual period occurs during the week the patch is not worn. Some women wear patches continuously, changing them every week. The patch is worn on the shoulder, the upper arm, the buttocks, or the abdomen.

The patch is safe and effective, and easily and rapidly reversible. Once-a-week dosing removes some of the anxiety felt by women who sometimes question whether they have remembered to take their daily pill. The patch provides many of the same noncontraceptive health benefits of combined estrogen-progestin birth control pills.

Since the patch is worn externally, it cannot always be concealed, which causes a privacy issue for some women. As with all hormonal forms of contraception, there is no protection against sexually transmitted diseases. In addition to the side effects that can be associated with all hormonal contraceptives, about 20% of patch users experience a skin rash at the site of administration.

Patches also may become fully or partially detached. If a patch becomes detached, it can often be pressed down to reattach it. If all the edges do not stick tightly to the skin, the patch should be replaced with a new one, but only for the amount of time the first patch should have remained on the skin, so as to not disrupt the cycle. If a patch has been or may have been partially or fully detached for more than 24 hours, a backup form of contraception should be used for the next seven days.

VAGINAL RING

NuvaRing® is a flexible plastic ring containing hormones similar to those in birth control pills and Ortho-Evra®. It is placed inside the vagina for three weeks, then removed during the fourth week and a menstrual period usually occurs during that week. If the ring is accidentally removed before the fourth week, it can be re-inserted within three hours.

Hormone levels that suppress ovulation occur within one day of inserting the ring, so there is no need to use a second form of contraception at the beginning of the cycle, as there is when birth control pills are first being used. However, if the ring falls out during the three weeks of use and is out of the body for more than three hours, a backup form of contraception should be used for seven days.

Once-a-month administration provides a relatively long period of protection. Self-insertion provides privacy and ease of use; there is no need to make a medical appointment. Since the ring is worn internally, there is a high degree of privacy about contraceptive use. Privacy is compromised to some degree because the rings are sold in multiple packets, and should be stored in a refrigerator until used, although they can be stored at room temperature for up to three months.

In a study comparing the NuvaRing® with birth control pills containing 30 mcg EE and 0.15 mg levonorgestrel, the NuvaRing® provided significantly more cycle control, with little spotting. Satisfaction is also high, with few women suffering side effects, and few women noting any sensation of the ring being in place, even during intercourse. In addition to the side effects that may occur with use of any hormonal contraceptive method, users of the ring also had some cases of vaginal discomfort from local irritation, and some had vaginal discharge.

If a woman switches from combined estrogen-progestin birth control pills to the NuvaRing®, she should insert the ring on the day she would start a new packet of pills. If she is switching from progestin-only pills, she should insert the ring on the same day she takes her last pill.

IUD

Intrauterine devices (IUDs) were a common method of birth control in the United States in the 1970s, but fell out of favor, mostly due to a high incidence of upper-genital-tract infections, many of which led to pelvic inflammatory disease (PID) and sterility (inability to conceive). However, many experts today believe that IUDs may come to be popular once again in the near future. Levonorgestrel-releasing IUDs have been tested and found to be both safe and effective when used properly in a population of women for whom IUDs are an appropriate choice for contraception (Figure 5.2).

In addition to blocking ovulation, progestin-only IUDs provide the same non-contraceptive benefits as other progestin-only formulations, such as pills, Depo-Provera® injections, and implants. Side effects are the same as any other progestin-only form of contraception.

Hormone-containing IUDs must be placed by a healthcare provider—they cannot be self-inserted like vaginal rings. For some women, this is a drawback of the method, but it can in reality be positive, since the woman receives regular health care.

There are two major advantages to IUDs. First, once inserted, an IUD can remain in place for months or even years, constantly releasing a low level of progestin into the

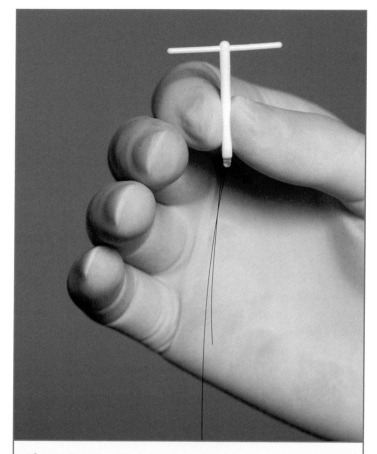

Figure 5.2 An IUD is a small, T-shaped device with a string attached to one end. It is placed inside the uterus to prevent pregnancy.

bloodstream to suppress ovulation. Second, an IUD is immediately reversible: once it is removed, hormone levels in the blood go back to a neutral level almost immediately.

IMPLANT

Implanon® is a single 4-centimeter-long contraceptive usually implanted in a woman's upper arm, which releases a constant

daily flow of 60 mcg of the progestin etongestrel. An Implanon®
implant provides contraceptive protection for three full years.
Blood levels of etongestrel sufficient to suppress ovulation are
reached within 24 hours of surgical implantation. Contraceptive
protection is immediately reversed when Implanon® is removed.

Implanon® replaces an older implant method, Norplant®,
which provided up to five years of protection. While Norplant®
implantation is no longer performed, the last Norplant® users
will not have their implants removed until some time in 2008.

There are two major benefits of hormonal implants for
contraception. First, they are effective for a long time—three
years for Implanon® and five years for Norplant®. This has
proved to be important for many women, especially those who
live chaotic lives and have difficulty keeping up with hormonal
birth control systems that require daily use (pills) or even
weekly use (patches). For women who have trouble accessing a
health-care provider, even the three months of protection
afforded by Depo-Provera® is often difficult to maintain. A single minor surgical procedure that provides three years of birth
control can create a major improvement in quality of life. Second, because there is no room for user error, the system is
essentially 100% effective.

In a study conducted in Colorado among teenage and
young mothers covered by Medicaid, about 30% chose Nor-
plant® as their method of birth control. Their repeat birth rate
was 2.5% after two years, compared with 22.1% for teens who
chose another contraceptive method. Since only 84% of women
continued to use Norplant® after one year, it can be assumed
that most of those births were to mothers who voluntarily discontinued use. However, Norplant® was shown in studies to
cause breakthrough ovulation, especially among women who
weighed over 153 pounds. No pregnancies occurred in over
70,000 cycles of Implanon during the product's research phase.

Of course, such positives can be turned into negatives if
the technology is used in a callous way. Many advocates for

women, children, and disadvantaged families protested early use of Norplant® by doctors, arguing that the providers were using Norplant® for their convenience rather than for young women's health. A single visit in five years for birth control meant that a doctor or nurse practitioner did not have to see a teenager or young adult regularly and did not have the opportunity to counsel her about family planning or about proper health care.

As is the case with the reintroduction of IUDs into the contraceptive mix, health-care providers are now being educated by their professional associations about the importance of patient selection, truly informed patient consent, and proper follow-up for women who utilize hormone implants. They must screen patients to see for whom an implant is an appropriate birth control method. And they must educate and counsel their patients correctly about not only proper use of the technology (making sure it remains implanted until removed by a health-care provider), but also that the technology does not protect against sexually transmitted diseases, and that it is easily reversible, should the woman decide at a later time that she wishes to conceive.

6

Is Hormonal Contraception Right for You?

Family planning is the most intimate decision a couple makes in their lives together. Sexual intimacy is an important and healthy aspect of a committed relationship. For a couple in a committed, long-term relationship, the decision on when to try to have children is bound up with decisions about education, occupations and careers, and where to live. And the decision about what method of birth control to use is a decision that has a dramatic impact on their lives.

Today, the vast majority of contraceptive technology puts the responsibility for contraception on the woman. To be sure, part of that is rooted in the history of the power relationship between men and women, but much of it is also a result of biology. While many women in both industrialized and developing countries have decried the burden of responsibility for contraception, increasingly women are seeing their role as the primary responsible party for both contraception and disease prevention as an important aspect in their own self-determination.

The question of whether female hormonal contraception is appropriate is important for each young woman to consider (Figure 6.1). A discussion of the pros and cons of birth control pills should take place with a young woman's parents and/or her health-care

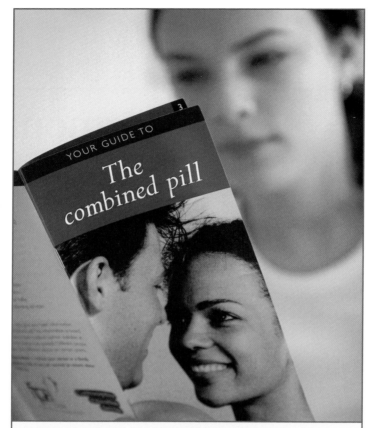

Figure 6.1 When considering birth control pills, it is important to ask as many questions as possible. Parents and health-care professionals are always good resources. Web sites dedicated to health topics can also be good sources for information.

provider, be that a private doctor or a clinician at a school or community health clinic.

The question for each young woman is essentially, "Is the pill or some other hormonal contraceptive delivery system the right choice for me?" This book cannot answer that question; only the reader, with input from trusted and knowledgeable advisors, can answer it. The facts on which to base a decision, however, are these:

- Female hormonal contraception, when used correctly, is the most effective means of birth control short of a surgical procedure to make either the girl/woman or her male sexual partner unable to produce a child (tubal ligation for a female, vasectomy for a male).

- Female hormonal contraception, even when used correctly, does not protect against sexually transmitted diseases (STDs).

- The use of female hormonal contraception requires an open, honest, and ongoing relationship with a primary health-care provider. The doctor needs to know about the young woman's complete health history, including any underlying medical conditions that hormonal contraception could exacerbate, and medications (prescription or over-the-counter) that the young woman uses, whether she smokes or frequently uses alcohol, and whether she uses street drugs. The young woman must be open with her clinician about any mental health, emotional, or maturity issues that might get in the way of her remembering to take her pill, change her patch, or put in a new ring. The provider also must understand the conditions the young woman lives in: Are they stable or hectic? Is she able to take a pill at the same time every day? Does she have a safe relationship with her sexual partner and does he understand her decision to use hormonal contraception? She must feel that her health-care provider is someone she can talk to about the relationship dynamics that may have an impact on her ability to maintain the regimen necessary for the method to be effective.

- Especially in the case of teenagers, can she handle the "social" impact of using hormonal contraception? In some cultures and social groups, pill use is still seen as a negative. Can she put aside any remarks she may hear in the school hallway, on the street, or at her house of worship about rumors that she is "loose" or "easy" because someone has told someone that she is on the pill?

- At the bottom line, while there are health risks associated with use of birth control pills and other hormonal contraceptive methods, any health risks pale in comparison with the health risks involved for women, especially for teens and for women in less-developed countries, of pregnancy and childbirth

FIVE QUESTIONS TO ASK BEFORE USING BIRTH CONTROL PILLS

1. Should I use the pill or should I use another method of birth control?

The decision is up to you, but it should be made in conjunction with at least one adult with whom you have a close relationship, most likely a parent and/or your health-care provider. True, using the birth control pill means that you don't have to "think about" birth control in the immediate time around engaging in sex. But it also means that you must remember to take your pills every day in order for them to be effective. And birth control pills do not guard against sexually transmitted diseases (STDs), such as syphilis, gonorrhea, chlamydia, herpes, HIV, or human papillomavirus. If you are going to have sex, you should engage in safe sex practices.

2. What happens if I miss taking a pill?

That depends on what you mean by "miss" taking a pill. If you normally take your birth control pill in the evening but forget, you may take one the next morning and another at your regular time the next night and they will continue to be fully effective. If you miss two days in a row, you may take two pills a day (morning and evening) for two days, but you must also use another, backup form of contraception for seven days until your hormonal cycle is back on track. If you miss three or more pills, you should stop taking them, use another form of contraception until your next menstrual period, then begin a new pill cycle.

3. What are the advantages of bicycling, tricycling, or using a 91-pill packet?

This is purely a personal choice. There are no differences in effectiveness. Many women feel most comfortable having a regular, monthly menstrual cycle, while others like the convenience of only having a menstrual period every two or three months. Teens and young women who use birth control pills for control of severe acne or for treatment of polycystic ovary syndrome (PCOS), which are both medically approved uses, generally use a 28-day cycle.

4. What happens if I am having side effects like headaches, nausea, bloating and weight gain, or breakthrough bleeding when I should not be having a period?

First, don't worry. Side effects are relatively common, especially in the first few months of use. Second, call your health-care provider when the problem starts. Don't let it persist and make you anxious or worried. Depending on what side effects you are experiencing, your health-care provider may change your birth control pill prescription to a different formulation. There are many to choose from that use different formulations of the synthetic hormones and in different amounts. There are some women who cannot use any formulation of birth control pills because these symptoms persist no matter what form they try. Some of these women may be able to use a different delivery route for hormonal contraception, such as an injection, patch, vaginal ring, or infused intrauterine device, because the chemicals enter the bloodstream without going through the intestine.

5. What if I become ill and have to take some other kind of medication like antibiotics?

Before beginning birth control pills, you need to discuss with your health-care provider any other medications you regularly take. Your doctor must take these into account when prescribing the appropriate birth control pill formulation for you. Birth control pills have interactions with many different medications: the other medication may become less effective or the birth control pills may become less effective. If the person who prescribes your birth control pill is not your primary care provider (for instance, if you see a gynecologist for sexual and reproductive health care and a pediatrician or internist for general health care), you must keep the two of them current on what medications you use. Any time you see your general care provider for an illness, you need to remind him or her that you are using birth control pills, and what formulation you use.

Glossary

Anemia (iron-deficiency anemia)—A reduced level of red blood cells caused by a lack of iron in the system, often a symptom of heavy menstrual bleeding.

Bile—A yellow-green substance, manufactured in the liver and stored in the gallbladder, that helps break down fats in the digestive process.

Birth control patch—An adhesive patch, similar to a nicotine patch, worn for one week at a time to deliver a constant flow of the same hormones (estrogen and progestin) found in combined birth control pills.

Birth control pill—An oral contraceptive containing either the hormones estrogen and progestin (combined pills) or only progestin (progestin-only pills), taken daily, which has three mechanisms of action: to stop ovulation, to thicken the cervical mucus and inhibit sperm from entering the uterus, and to inhibit fertilization of an egg by sperm.

Centers for Disease Control and Prevention (CDC)—The United States federal agency that monitors the health status of Americans.

Cervix—The area of the female reproductive tract that sits at the top of the vagina and the bottom of the uterus.

Cholesterol—A fat-soluble liquid that is a component of animal fats and synthesized in the body. Deposits of cholesterol that harden and adhere to the walls of veins and arteries lead to narrowing and reduced blood flow. Deposits in the gallbladder form gallstones.

Contraceptive—A medication or device that keeps conception from occurring.

Deep Vein Thrombosis (DVT)—Also known as thromboembolism; a condition in which a blood clot forms in the large veins, especially in the leg. A DVT that breaks off and travels to the lungs can be fatal.

Depo-Provera®—A highly effective, injected form of progestin-only hormonal birth control given every 12 weeks.

Diastolic—The pressure of blood moving through the artery when the heart's ventricles relax between heartbeats.

Dysmenorrhea—A painful menstrual period.

Ectopic pregnancy—A leading cause of female infertility, this occurs when an egg is fertilized and cells begin to divide while still in the fallopian tube, causing a blockage of the tube.

Endometrial cancer—Cancer of the lining of the uterus.

Estrogen—The primary female sex hormone; one or another synthetic form of estrogen is combined with synthetic progesterone (progestin) in combined hormonal birth control, delivered by pill, patch, or vaginal ring.

Fallopian tubes—The structures that run from the ovaries to the uterus in the female reproductive system.

False positive—A result of a medical test that shows something to be true when it actually isn't. For example, an electrocardiogram (EKG) reading could indicate that a heart attack has occurred when in reality one of the lead wires was not attached correctly, thereby interrupting the electrical signal and causing an inaccurate reading.

Fertilization—The point at which sperm joins with an egg, signaling conception.

Food and Drug Administration (FDA)—The federal agency that must approve all new medications and medical devices before they can be sold to Americans.

Gallstones—Deposits of cholesterol that form in the gallbladder, leading to pain.

Hormone—A naturally occurring substance produced in one body organ that stimulates or regulates the activity of another organ or body system.

Implant (contraceptive implant)—A progestin-only hormonal contraceptive implanted under the skin that provides continuous-release contraceptive protection for three years.

Insulin—A hormone manufactured in the pancreas that regulates absorption of sugars so they can be used for energy. Inability to manufacture enough insulin, or the inability of the body to utilize insulin, results in diabetes mellitus.

Intrauterine device (IUD)—The current generation of IUDs provides a constant release of a progestin-only contraceptive formulation while in place in the uterus.

Menstrual cycle—The period of approximately 28 days during which a woman undergoes ovulation and a series of hormonal changes that affect fertility.

Menstrual period—The period of approximately five to seven days at the end of each menstrual cycle, characterized by bleeding and the shedding of cells of the uterine lining.

Oral contraceptives—Birth control pills.

Ovarian cancer—Cancer of the ovaries; use of birth control pills for 10 years or more has been shown in studies to reduce the risk of ovarian cancer.

Plan B®—The trade name for emergency contraception, a high-dose combined birth control formulation that can be taken within 72 hours after unprotected sex to greatly reduce the risk of pregnancy.

Progestin—A synthetic version of the female sex hormone progesterone; it is used in both combined (estrogen-progestin) and progestin-only birth control pills. Progestin-only formulations are also delivered by implant, vaginal ring, and intrauterine device.

Systolic—Systolic pressure is the pressure exerted by blood on the walls of arteries when the heart's ventricles contract.

Uterus—The portion of the female reproductive system where the fertilized egg implants after conception and develops through gestation.

Vaginal ring—A soft, plastic ring inserted in the vagina that provides three weeks of constant-release progestin-only contraceptive protection.

World Health Organization (WHO)—United Nations agency charged with monitoring and improving the health conditions of the world's population. It is active in promoting healthy family planning, including education about and provision of contraceptive methods, as well as maternal and child health care, in less-developed countries.

Bibliography

Books and Articles

Blackburn, R.D., J.A. Cunkelman, and V.M. Zlidar. *Oral Contraceptives—An Update. Population Reports, Series A, No. 9.* Baltimore, MD: Johns Hopkins University School of Public Health, Population Information Program, 2000.

Djerassi, Carl. *The Pill, Pygmy Chimps, and Degas' Horse: The Autobiography of Carl Djerassi.* New York: Basic Books, 1992.

Harris, Gardiner. "U.S. Again Delays Decision on Sale of Next-Day Pill." *New York Times* (August 27, 2005).

Harris, Gardiner. "Drugs, Politics, and the F.D.A." *New York Times* (August 28, 2005).

Harris, Gardiner. "Official Quits on Pill Delay at the F.D.A." *New York Times* (September 1, 2005).

Icon Health Publications. *Birth Control Pills: A Medical Dictionary, Bibliography, and Annotated Research Guide to Internet References.* San Diego, CA: Icon Health, 2003.

Web Sites

"Contraception/Birth Control." Center for Young Women's Health, Children's Hospital Boston. www.youngwomenshealth.org.

"Depo-Provera Hormonal Injections." Center for Young Women's Health, Children's Hospital Boston. www.youngwomenshealth.org.

"Medical Use of the Oral Contraceptive Pill: A Guide for Teens." Center for Young Women's Health, Children's Hospital Boston. www.youngwomenshealth.org.

"Pros and Cons of Different Methods of Birth Control." Center for Young Women's Health, Children's Hospital Boston. www.youngwomenshealth.org.

"The Hormone Patch- (Ortho-Evra)." Center for Young Women's Health, Children's Hospital Boston. www.youngwomenshealth.org.

"The Vaginal Hormonal Ring (NuvaRing)." Center for Young Women's Health, Children's Hospital Boston. www.youngwomenshealth.org.

Further Reading

Connell, Elizabeth B. *The Contraception Sourcebook.* Chicago: Contemporary Books, 2002.

Edelson, Paula. *Straight Talk About Teenage Pregnancy.* New York: Facts On File, 1998.

Knowles, John, and Marcia Ringel. *All About Birth Control: A Personal Guide.* New York: Three Rivers Press, 1998.

Stanley, Deborah. *Sexual Health Information for Teens: Health Tips About Sexual Development, Human Reproduction, and Sexually Transmitted Diseases.* Detroit, MI: Omnigraphics, 2003.

Web Sites

Center for Communications Programs, Johns Hopkins School of Public Health
www.infoforhealth.org

Center for Young Women's Health, Children's Hospital Boston
www.youngwomenshealth.org

Feminist Women's Health Center/Cedar River Clinics
www.fwhc.org

National Library of Medicine, National Institutes of Health
www.nlm.nih.gov/medline

National Women's Health Information Center
www.4winab,giv.faq.burtgcibt.gtn

Planned Parenthood Federation of America
www.plannedparenthood.org/pp2/portal/

U.S. National Library of Medicine and the National Institutes of Health
www.nlm.nih.gov/medlineplus/birthcontrol.html

Index

pregnancy, 16–17, 21,
33–34
Prelone, 28
premenstrual syndrome
(PMS), 26, 34, 36–37
Principen®, 28
progestin
breast cancer and, 66
Depo-Provera and, 70
drug interactions and,
28
in early pills, 12
endometrial cancer and,
37
intrauterine devices
and, 75
mechanism of action
and, 17–21
in modern pills, 13–14
seizures ans, 72
protease inhibitors, 28
Prozac®, 29
pulmonary embolisms,
51

regularity, 36–37
retrospective studies, 45
rheumatoid arthritis, 41
rhythm method, 16–17
rifampicin, 28–29
risks. *See also* side effects
breast cancer and,
65–67
carbohydrate metabo-
lism and, 52–54
cervical cancer and,
61–64

chlamydia and pelvic
inflammatory disease
and, 57–58
deep vein thrombosis
as, 50–53
drug interactions and,
27–29, 72
early pills and, 12–13
gallbladder disease and,
54–55
heart attacks as, 45–46
high blood pressure as,
52
human immunodefi-
ciency virus (HIV)
and, 59–61
liver cancer and, 67
liver tumors and, 55–56
migraine headaches as,
48–50
overview of, 24–27,
43–45, 56, 68
reproductive tract infec-
tions and, 57
stroke as, 46–48
RU-486, 20, 22–23

safety, 11–12, 23
Seasonale, 24
seizures, 72
sexually transmitted dis-
eases, 24, 57–64, 81
side effects, 12–13, 23,
83–84
smoking, 43, 45, 46, 48
Solfoton®, 27
spacer pills, 22–23

sperm motility, 18–19
sponges, 71
start date, 24
statistics, 10
steroids, oral, 28
stroke, 13, 26–27, 46–48
syphilis, 60

technology, developments
in, 71
Tegretol®, 27
therapeutic value, 11
Third world nations,
31–33, 36
thromboembolism, 50–53
thrombosis, 50–53
tricycling, 24, 83
tuberculosis, 28–29

uterus, 15

vaccines, HPV, 65
vaginal rings, 20–21,
74–75
vaginitis, 61
vasectomies, 71
vitamins, 41

warfarin, 28
weight gain, Depo-
Provera® and, 70

yeast infections, 61

Picture Credits

Trademark

About the Author

Laurel Shader, M.D., is chair of pediatrics at the Fair Haven Community Health Center in New Haven, Connecticut, and clinical assistant professor at Yale University School of Medicine and Yale University School of Nursing.

Jon Zonderman, her husband, is an independent writer and editor who specializes in health care, science and technology, and business.

About the Editor

David J. Triggle is a University Professor and a Distinguished Professor in the School of Pharmacy and Pharmaceutical Sciences at the State University of New York at Buffalo. He studied in the United Kingdom and earned his B.Sc. degree in Chemistry from the University of Southampton and a Ph.D. degree in Chemistry at the University of Hull. Following post-doctoral work at the University of Ottawa in Canada and the University of London in the United Kingdom, he assumed a position at the School of Pharmacy at Buffalo. He served as Chairman of the Department of Biochemical Pharmacology from 1971 to 1985 and as Dean of the School of Pharmacy from 1985 to 1995. From 1995 to 2001 he served as the Dean of the Graduate School, and as the University Provost from 2000 to 2001. He is the author of several books dealing with the chemical pharmacology of the autonomic nervous system and drug-receptor interactions, some 400 scientific publications, and has delivered over 1,000 lectures worldwide on his research.